PRAISE FOR MANDY HALE AND *YOU ARE ENOUGH*

"I love Mandy for being transparent enough to go deep into the hidden places we don't want anyone to see. Baring her flaws, her hurts, and her soul gives me the courage to face the imperfect things I hide behind my smile. Mandy is the only author I know who fearlessly tackles the question *Why are we still single?* She goes beyond the tired clichés and gets to the root of the problem and shows you how to get back up even when you constantly get knocked down. The words coming from Mandy's heart are like a soothing balm. Thank you for showing me that no matter what, I am enough."

—Sherri Shepherd, actress, comedian, Emmy Award–winning talk show host, and *New York Times* bestselling author

"Even though Mandy is known by millions for being the inspirational voice for single women, this book is a must-read for all adults, regardless of their marital status. In her unique, heartfelt, and authentic way, she shares her latest emotional journey in the pursuit of true love and personal fulfillment and reminds us that stumbling, crying, doubting, thinking, laughing, and learning along the way is expected. It's real, which means you're real—and that you have been, and always will be, enough."

—Amy Capetta, health and wellness writer

"Mandy's words are empowering and inspiring. She acknowledges that adversity is something we all face—but by accepting and loving who we are, we can overcome any personal obstacle we encounter."
—Derrick Levasseur, TV personality and author
of *The Undercover Edge*

"In a world where we are often subjected to the carefully curated, seemingly perfect version of other people's lives, Mandy Hale's YOU ARE ENOUGH takes us on a journey of self-discovery that is powerful and refreshingly authentic! Her story is equal parts relatable and inspiring, and I hope every woman who has ever had a moment of self-doubt (most of us) has the chance to read this book so that it can serve as a beautiful reminder that they are indeed (more than) enough!"
—Devyn Simone, TV host, dating coach, and matchmaker

"Mandy has done it again: YOU ARE ENOUGH is a timely and timeless reminder to women everywhere that you are fearfully and wonderfully made. That you alone are good enough: with a spouse, without a spouse, it does not matter. And that truly, once you love you, and know your value...everyone else around you will know the same."
—Sophia A. Nelson, award-winning NBC journalist
and bestselling author of *The Woman Code*

"Wow! What a beautiful, brave, and inspiring book. Mandy Hale has been through it all—heartbreak, loss, self-doubt, questioning of all she held dear—and has come out so much stronger and more beautiful on the other side. Her journey inspired me to remember that, yes, I too am enough! Any woman who has weathered dark times in her life (and who hasn't?) will find a kindred spirit in Mandy and great comfort in her words."

—Francesca Hogi, life and love coach

"I think sometimes people are afraid to be real with their readers. I think they want to help us but aren't willing to share their *entire* journey. This book is so refreshing. I finally see someone's complete process and I find so much of myself in there. I finally see the beauty of the journey and I realize the freedom in Mandy's honesty. Because of that, I am truly able to see that through it all, I am enough. As a single woman, I am SO grateful for Mandy's transparency. It's real, raw, and inspiring! This book easily connects to so many of us who have been or are going through some of the same things. It's amazing to be reminded that, through it all, you are enough!"

—Melinda Doolittle, singer, author, and TV personality

"This book literally made me both smile and cry. But mostly it made me feel *understood*. Less alone in this world. Mandy Hale writes in the voice of a dear, kind friend, filled with encouragement and urging the courage we all need to soldier on in life. Everyone's circumstances are unique, but YOU ARE ENOUGH contains a strong message of not giving up no matter who you are or where you are in life. I will be recommending this book to everyone!"

—Beth Harbison, *New York Times* bestselling author

YOU ARE
enough

HEARTBREAK, HEALING, AND BECOMING WHOLE

MANDY HALE

New York   Nashville

FaithWords
Hachette Book Group
1290 Avenue of the Americas, New York, NY 10104
faithwords.com
twitter.com/faithwords

First Edition: October 2018

FaithWords is a division of Hachette Book Group, Inc. The FaithWords name and logo are trademarks of Hachette Book Group, Inc.

The publisher is not responsible for websites (or their content) that are not owned by the publisher.

The Hachette Speakers Bureau provides a wide range of authors for speaking events. To find out more, go to www.hachettespeakersbureau.com or call (866) 376-6591.

Scriptures noted (MSG) are taken from *The Message*. Copyright © 1993, 1994, 1995, 1996, 2000, 2001, 2002. Used by permission of NavPress Publishing Group.

Scriptures noted (NIV) are taken from the Holy Bible, New International Version®, NIV®. Copyright © 1973, 1978, 1984, 2011 by Biblica, Inc.™ Used by permission of Zondervan. All rights reserved worldwide. www.zondervan.com. The "NIV" and "New International Version" are trademarks registered in the United States Patent and Trademark Office by Biblica, Inc.™

Library of Congress Cataloging-in-Publication Data has been applied for.

ISBNs: 978-1-5460-1234-4 (hardcover), 978-1-5460-1236-8 (ebook), 978-1-5460-3517-6 (B&N Black Friday signed edition), 978-1-5460-3516-9 (BN.com signed edition)

Printed in the United States of America

LSC-C

10 9 8 7 6 5 4 3 2 1

*For anyone who has ever wondered if you
matter, if your life serves a purpose, or if you
are enough:
You do. It does. YOU ARE.
Keep going. Keep going. Keep going.
You are a semicolon; you are not a period.*

contents

contents

introduction

Enough.

What a concept.

Fitting. Sufficient. Adequate. Acceptable. Complete. Not lacking. ENOUGH.

Whatever that sense of "okayness" is that some people are born with—well, I've never had it. I've never felt like I quite measured up to everyone else. From the time I was a little girl, I struggled with not feeling worthy: worthy of friendships, of opportunities, of love. (The great irony being that my full name means "worthy-of-love princess.")

This sense of lack has followed me my entire life and has impacted me in both negative and positive ways. Negatively, because it's led to me choosing wrong people to love and staying in friendships and situations that were not honoring to me, long after I should have walked away. Positively, because when you carry around an innate sense of unworthiness, you tend to hustle for your worth. Work a little harder than everyone else just to prove that you are valuable, you are important, you are ENOUGH. In that respect, my constant need to prove myself has made me a go-getter, and some incredible career opportunities have come to me as a result of my tenacity.

But through it all—even when working alongside Oprah and speaking at the biggest church in the country and hitting the *New York Times* best-seller list—I carried around this shadow of lack and insecurity and unworthiness. This taunting, cruel shadow that was always one step behind me, making sure to remind me that no matter how far I rose in life, I would never rise high enough to outrun it. I would never really "earn my stripes." I would never be ENOUGH.

Then...I wound up in a mental hospital, and everything changed.

A mental hospital. Let's keep it real, folks. By society's standards (not mine), this is possibly the very lowest of the low places. And although I have experienced it first-hand and know that the people within those walls are some of the best I've ever encountered, those who have no experience with mental illness or depression or treatment or recovery view it with fear and judgment and even distaste. We as a people have a habit of coping with things we don't understand with defense mechanisms like mockery and criticism and cruelty. (Which is incredibly unfortunate and a tendency that we, collectively, as humans, need to fight with everything we have.)

The prior year of my life leading up to the mental hospital was without a doubt the most disappointing and challenging and heartbreaking year. Up to that point, I had prided myself, as many people do, on an ability to bounce back. To "roll with the punches." To get back up and try, try again. But somewhere in the midst of family tragedy and career disappointment and relationship failures, I lost my ability to persevere. I lost the essence of who I was. It was all mired in the "life-i-ness" of life. I simply woke up one morning and couldn't take another step.

So that's how I found myself—a writer whose message was all about inspiration and hope and positivity—completely bereft of all of those things and struggling to get out of bed and live my life. Struggling to the point where I had to enroll in an intensive outpatient program at a mental hospital for crippling anxiety and depression.

Rock bottom, it would seem.

But, as it turns out, it was that very rock bottom that became the firmest foundation I had ever planted my feet on. A foundation so solid it finally provided the springboard I needed to outrun that teasing, taunting shadow of unworthiness that had followed me my entire life.

Sometimes it takes getting pushed to the very edge

before you can find your voice and courage to speak out again. Sometimes it takes hitting that rock bottom to realize you're done descending and it's time to rise. Sometimes it takes being told you're nothing—being made to feel like you're nothing—to help you see that you are complete.

YOU. ARE. ENOUGH.

You see, sometimes you have to realize that you've HAD enough to realize that you ARE enough.

Over these past two years, I've seen just how closely those two principles are intertwined: the rock bottom and the soaring heights...the valley and the mountaintop...the agony of defeat and the thrill of victory. How sometimes it takes great heartbreak to find great healing and even greater wholeness. How being told how unworthy you are of great love and happiness and beauty and light can actually help you see once and for all just how worthy you really are. Just how deserving you are of the things and the life that you dream of and hope for, and how nothing you could ever do or not do takes away from your worthiness or your "enoughness."

Over the course of a year and a half, I descended into total darkness. I was told I never meant anything to someone I'd loved for a decade. I lost people I loved—one, tragically, to suicide. I had my heart broken more than once. I sat in total silence in front of a blank screen for hours on end, waiting for words to pour out of me that seemed would never come. I questioned everything about myself: my faith, my judgment, my friendships, my career path, my worth, my value, my purpose. My LIFE.

But through it all, I'm still standing.

I'm still here.

I'm bruised, banged-up, significantly more guarded than I was two years ago, more realistic than idealistic these days... but I'm still here. The doubt, the fear, the heartbreak, the depression, the anxiety, the insecurity: It didn't win. The people who hurt me and let me down: They didn't win. The disappointment and the failure, and the hopes and deferred dreams: Nope. They didn't win either.

I've always struggled with feeling like I was ENOUGH. Enough for love interests. Enough for my former publisher. Enough for my family and friends and readers and myself, and, yes... even God.

But over this past year and a half, I've been in the midst of painful, beautiful transformation. A journey of heartbreak. A journey of healing. And a journey of becoming WHOLE. A journey I now want to invite you on with me.

I'm finally learning to accept myself as I am. Learning to like myself as I am. Learning to like and accept my life as it is. Learning to stop begging people to want me or love me or make me feel like I'm ENOUGH. And learning that it's okay to stand up and say: I've had ENOUGH. I've had enough of hustling for my worth. I've had enough of groveling to people unworthy of me for scraps of love or time or attention. I've had enough of keeping people in my life who diminish me. And I've had enough of trying to be anything other than me...because I, in all my imperfect, messy glory, am perfectly ENOUGH.

Have you had enough? And are you ready to declare that YOU ARE ENOUGH?

A few months ago, I made my declaration of enoughness official, with my best friend from group therapy by my side. Someone I didn't know a year ago but who is now my sister for life, all thanks to the brokenness that brought us together. I tattooed the word "enough" on my wrist...a way of branding myself, I suppose, for those days when my worthiness tank feels a little low. So now when I start to forget how ENOUGH I am, I can just look down at my wrist and look from side to side at the people next to me, doing this wild and beautiful and difficult life thing with me, and *remember*. Remember this season of my life. Remember these precious moments of struggle and surrender and fighting to become the person I'm meant to be. Remember that I might not be exactly who and where I want to be but that I'm taking steps every day to get there.

I am ENOUGH. And you are enough.

Sometimes we just need a little reminder.

I hope this book will be that reminder for you.

It's not always going to be pretty. It's not as light-hearted and happy and shiny as some of my previous work. We're going to get real and raw and gritty within these pages. Because life isn't always lighthearted and happy and shiny, and it's okay to admit that. Some chapters of our lives are going to be darker than others, and it's okay to admit that.

Sometimes you've gotta get a little lost in order to get found. And it's okay to admit that.

If you've had enough of being lost, of being sad, of being depressed, of being hurt and scared and downtrodden and anxious and alone...this book is for you.

If you've always felt like you never quite measured up...this book is for you.

If you're ready to make your own declaration of enoughness...this book is for you.

If you are heartbroken, if you're in search of healing, if you're struggling with everything you have to gather your missing pieces back together into something that even slightly resembles wholeness...this book is for you.

If you've come to the end of yourself, I hope this book will be your new beginning. Just as it's my new beginning. We're taking this journey together. Declaring that we've had enough and we are enough. Overcoming our heartbreak. Claiming our healing. Stepping into our wholeness.

Let's get started.

YOU ARE *enough*

chapter 1

WHEN YOU LOSE YOURSELF, YOU FIND YOURSELF

*W*hen you lose yourself, you find yourself." Seven words, spoken to me in passing by a smiling man on a sidewalk during my daily walk.

He wasn't really dressed for exercising...or even for the heat. He wore street clothes, not workout gear, and a wool stocking cap in the eighty-something-degree weather. He had the biggest smile on his face.

I took a walk almost every single day down beautiful tree-lined Main Street...and I'd never seen the man before.

When you lose yourself, you find yourself. Just those seven words, delivered with a great big grin in response to the neighborly hello I uttered to him in passing. He didn't explain himself. He just kept walking. And I kept walking...shaking my head in wonder as I continued down the street, on my way home.

The man couldn't possibly know that I had been in a season of feeling lost, stuck, unsure about what was next for me. How I'd literally written in my journal (more than a few times) the sentence *Jesus, help me find myself again.* Asking Him to help me find the Mandy who was idealistic, who found enchantment and wonder and inspiration everywhere, who believed that absolutely anything was possible, and who, I daresay, even had a touch of magic running through her veins. To help me find the Mandy that I used to be...the one who had simple, childlike faith. The one who, as a child, was constantly singing or humming, because I found life so utterly delightful that I had joy overflowing and just had to open up my mouth to let it all come tumbling out.

The one who still dared to imagine that fairy tales could and do come true. The one who existed before life came in and got hard, before a string of heartbreaks caused me to view love through a much less hopeful lens than before, before I dismissed my fairy-tale dreams and childlike enthusiasm as "kid stuff" and hung it up on the shelf to gather dust, relegated to the same spot as my ballet shoes and my Barbie dolls and my Uno cards.

The man in the stocking cap also couldn't see into the future...could he? He couldn't see how my footsteps that were carrying me so assuredly down Main Street today would carry me to depths I never dreamed I'd fall tomorrow.

How within a month, my family would face the most traumatic, gut-wrenching season we'd ever encountered as my brother-in-law lost his leg and almost his life. How within weeks after that, I'd lose my publisher of four years, my confidence, and even my religion.

And the year after that, the love of my life. Within hours of losing my precious grandmother. And a few months before losing a dear friend to suicide.

He couldn't possibly know that the next year and a half of my life would be shrouded in loss and heartbreak and questioning everything I'd ever known and a dark night of the soul like nothing I had ever experienced before.

The man on the street in the stocking cap couldn't possibly know these things.

Or could he?

When you lose yourself, you find yourself.

I'm not saying the man was an angel…but I'm not saying he wasn't.

All I know is, he was sent across my path to deliver a message that had already been formulating in my mind and my heart for quite some time. I just hadn't found a way to put it into words.

The man on the street in the stocking cap helped me find the words.

And I think, friends, he might have even helped me find my way. Or "unfind" my way, as the case may be.

Because over the next year and a half of my life, I

would lose myself and my way completely. I would lose friends and loved ones and ideals I held dear, and idealistic notions about life and parts of myself I would never get back...but I would also lose fear and self-doubt and pretense, and any need I ever had to be anything other than exactly who and what I was.

And I would find myself again. Not the same version of me that I was looking for, but a stronger version. A wiser version. A woman who knew that she was enough, just as she was. A woman who had been tried in the fire but, instead of being burned by it, came out gold.

A woman who, finally, after doubting and questioning and striving and hustling for her worth for years...finally, finally came to the realization that she was and is and always has been...

ENOUGH.

And every moment of every struggle and success and high and low and heartbreak and healing I would experience for the next year and a half was designed to bring me one step closer to that understanding.

All of that was coming. Not on this day, but it was coming.

And the man in the stocking cap on Main Street seemed to kick it all off. With a grin, and a knowing lope, he went about his way, and I went about mine.

A few moments later, when I turned to look back at him over my shoulder, he was gone.

And a few weeks later, the life I had come to know was gone, too.

You Are Enough

Because that's sort of the crux of this whole life thing: Nothing beyond the very moment we're living in is known, which can feel terrifying. There's no agenda here. No itinerary. We are often forced to take the step before we can even see the staircase. But in the midst of all that uncertainty and lack of clarity, there lies a wild beauty. A hope. Possibility. The promise of something bigger than us, happening just beneath the surface that we can't see. So when you're tempted to look for constant clarity and answers, just close your eyes and breathe and remind yourself that God knows what you're ready for. He knows what your arms are able to carry. He knows what your heart can contain. He knows what's coming, and He knows how and when to prepare you for it. He knows the right time, the right place, the right person, the right answer. He knows, so you don't have to. You're free to relax and let go, and, yes, maybe even lose yourself a little in order to find yourself, trusting that in His perfect way, in His perfect timing, all will become clear. And you will get through it. And you are enough, for whatever comes your way.

chapter 2

ONE MONDAY MORNING

You never expect the really big moments in life to arrive in the way they do. A middle-of-the-night phone call rarely brings good news. A middle-of-the-night phone call is, in fact, almost always expected to bring bad news. But a phone call on a very unassuming ordinary Monday morning? That's not the kind of phone call that tends to change your life.

Until it does.

A few weeks after the strange encounter with the gentleman on my morning walk, my mom called. Her voice was tearful and frantic. My brother-in-law, Kevin, had been in a bad car accident, she said. She had no idea about the severity of his injuries or even if he was still alive. My dad and my sister were on their way to him.

The memories of that day still come and go in painful flashes. I can see myself trying to throw on clothes while intermittently throwing myself on the floor before God to beg, to beseech, to humbly ask Him to spare my brother-in-law's life. "He has two little girls, God. He has two little girls. They need him. They need their daddy..."

Then, later, sitting with my mom, hands clasped, as my dad explained on speakerphone, his voice breaking, that the doctors were going to have to remove Kevin's leg to save his life. *Remove his leg. His leg.* My mom and I falling to our knees on the floor at the news. His leg, Lord. His leg. *My God. Oh, God...no. No. No...*

Holding my mom as she sobbed, listening to my dad choke on his own words as he tried to comfort us both. My dad was crying. My daddy, whom I've only seen cry a handful of times in my life...

Calling out to God silently and desperately as I held my mom: *I'm not enough for this, God. I'm not strong enough, I'm not together enough, I'm not brave enough to face this. I am not enough. We are not enough.*

Then, suddenly, from nowhere, I felt a supernatural strength. The straightening of my spine. The setting of my face like flint. A peace that surpassed all understanding. The tears stopped. The calm fell. As my mom wept in my arms, I felt God whisper: *I'm here. I'm with Kevin. I'm with all of you. I will never leave or forsake any of you. Trust me. Trust me. Trust me.*

And I did. It's funny: In seventeen years of being a Christ follower and hundreds of recitations of the Scripture "My grace is sufficient for you, for my power is made perfect in weakness" (2 Cor. 12:9 NIV), it wasn't until all strength was gone, taken, snuffed out in a moment of heartbreaking loss, that I fully grasped those words. *We are weak, God... so weak. So pitifully human. I don't know if we, as a family, are enough. I don't know if we can rise to the challenge of this.*

He whispered: *You're right, Mandy, you can't... but I CAN...*

And so I entered in and saw Him at work. Sitting my nieces down, eight and twelve, and telling them with as much positivity as I could muster that Daddy had been in an accident and wouldn't be coming home tonight. And neither would Mommy, because she had to be with Daddy. Watching their sweet little smiles crumble into heart-wrenching sobs as they asked: "Is Daddy going to die?"

Going to my sister's house and seeing the roast simmering in the Crock-Pot... ready for a family dinner that would never happen now. Folding Kevin's laundry and feeling my breath catch as I folded his left sock, and Emma taking her daddy's socks and putting them on her own feet to feel closer to him.

Watching my sister explain the full situation to Emma and Olivia later that night... "Daddy's leg was hurt really badly. It's going to look a little different now." And seeing understanding finally dawn on their sweet, sad faces as Olivia looked up at her mom and asked in a quivering voice: "Is Daddy going to have a bionic leg?"

The outpouring of love, from my sister's friends, her church, her coworkers, my dad's family, total strangers, was incredible: a Chick-fil-A employee leaning out the window at the drive-through and offering to pray for us; my niece's best friend giving her a book called *My Dad the Superhero*, about a daddy with a prosthetic leg; a friend of my sister's showing up to mow the yard without being asked; a friend of mine going in search of a new microwave because my sister's broke and we needed fast, easy meals. The list goes on and on and on.

Taking the girls to see their daddy for the first time after his accident and seeing the emotion on Kevin's face as he embraced his babies. Watching the looks of relief spread across their faces as they saw that their daddy was still their daddy. ("We think it's kinda cool that Daddy's going to have a bionic leg," they both agreed.)

The grace and courage with which Kevin handled and has continued to handle his new situation—perhaps the greatest grace and courage I've ever seen. The loving, nurturing, protective, brave, constant vigil my sister held by her husband's bedside. A living, breathing illustration of "in sickness and in health."

The phrase that kept going through my mind over and over during that first week of heartbreak and grace was "Jesus wept" (John 11:35 NIV). I think He wanted to remind me that it's okay for us to weep, too. To mourn. To grieve. But also to rejoice in what remains.

But for the grace of God, this part of my story could have ended very differently. Through everything we would go through, through everything I would go through, over the next year, there would be so many God winks...testimonies and touchstones...to let us know that He was always there, that He's present in our pain, that He hears and sees and feels right along with us. And I think that's really all we can ask for: a Savior who doesn't stand back and watch our suffering but who gets down in the midst of it with us.

Life changed forever for my brother-in-law on that ordinary Monday. It changed forever for my family. Just as it might have changed for you on your ordinary Monday. The day you lost your dad. The day you found the lump in your breast. The day the love of your life walked away from you.

But the good news is this: Through it all, God didn't change.

He never has.

He never will.

Whatever your ordinary Monday held, God held you tighter.

So we cling to that—and to Him—and we carry on.

You Are Enough

Watching my brother-in-law, Kevin, heal, learn to walk again, and accept his new situation with complete grace and courage revealed to me more than ever just how ENOUGH we are for whatever comes our way. And God reminded me over and over again in those days of healing and surrender just how faithful His provision and healing are. He's always there with us, in the midst of whatever it is we're going through. He never leaves us, never forsakes us, even when we go through seasons when we can't feel or see Him. He might not answer our prayers in the way or with the timing that we would like, but He loves us right through the process. Right through the heartbreak. Right through the healing. And right through the becoming whole. And in His presence, there is peace. Peace that there's nothing I can face, nothing my family can face, nothing YOU can face...that we aren't ENOUGH for. He's always there. In the doubting, in the worrying, in the questioning, in the triumph, and in the tragedy (especially then)...

HE IS ALWAYS THERE.

chapter 3

YOUR LIFE WILL BE DIFFERENT, BUT IT WILL BE AMAZING

My brother-in-law was at a ground zero in his life. He was learning to walk again. Learning to dress himself and shower and roll himself along in a wheelchair and to simply exist on this planet with one leg.

My family was at ground zero. The simple, easy life we had known before was gone. My sister was with Kevin at the hospital around the clock, so I was with the girls, essentially becoming a stand-in and often unsure-of-myself "mom." My mom and dad were supporting everyone as best they could. We were all in roles we'd never expected, doing things we'd never foreseen, feeling ill-equipped to handle this new life that had been thrust upon us.

And I was in the midst of my own ground zero. The tragedy that had unfolded in our lives had brought everything into focus for all of us and had served to stoke the fires of restlessness and uncertainty that I was feeling about my own life and career path. I didn't want to be a "brand" anymore. I just wanted to be myself. I just wanted to be Mandy. And I wanted that to be enough. I wanted to build a body of writing that mattered, that made a difference, that met people right where they were. Not a flashy, catchy, pithy brand made up of 140-character platitudes. And I felt like it was time to part ways with the publisher that had "discovered" me and that I had written three books with. I wanted to break free. I needed to break free. Going through the immense turmoil of the past weeks had taught me about the kind of person I wanted to be, the kind of friend and woman and writer I wanted to be. I felt like the person I saw myself becoming was bigger than the vision my publisher held for me or the box it wanted to keep me in.

In the midst of these ground-zero days, my niece Livi drew her daddy a picture. It was a portrait of her and her dad, sailing away together in a hot-air balloon, with words of encouragement written out in her messy little scrawl beside it: *Your life will be different, but it will be amazing.*

Oh, out of the mouths of babes.

As I sat, endlessly debating my own future as a writer, shaking in fear at the thought of striking out on my own, outside the umbrella of a publisher, my eight-year-old niece penned those simple and yet starkly profound words that helped me see that we are all at some form of ground zero in our lives. We are all feeling hopelessly ill-prepared and inadequate when it comes to the idea of striking out on our own and building something new. And it's up to us to be brave enough to climb into the basket of that hot-air balloon, knowing that it might look and feel entirely different from anything or any life we've experienced before, understanding that it might take us somewhere we never imagined we would go, but also realizing that it can still be really, really amazing. Life can still be really, really amazing even after the unimaginable happens.

I want to talk to you in the midst of your ground zero...whatever it may be. It doesn't have to be something as monumental as losing a limb or almost losing a family member to be life-altering. Perhaps you're going through a breakup. The person you thought was your forever walked away with no explanation, and now you're left picking up the pieces. Perhaps you lost your job and have no idea where next month's rent is coming from. Maybe a lifelong dream of yours has recently been snuffed out, leaving you questioning everything about your path and your purpose. Maybe you haven't heard from God in a really long time and you're starting to wonder if He cares...or if He even exists. (I get it. I've been there. And I'll be there again in just a couple of chapters.)

Here is what I want you to know. It's okay to hurt. It's

okay to cry. It's okay to ask questions (even of God). It's okay to yell and scream and feel, and even cuss if you need to. It's okay to be right where you're at, without trying to frantically search for the purpose that will come from your pain. or the message that will come from your mess. I'm finding that some pain doesn't serve a purpose. Sometimes pain is just pain...and we can let it be just that. We can feel it without trying to heal it. We can bring our fists down hard on all the feel-good singsong empty platitudes and send the pieces scattering right along with the shattered pieces of our hearts. WE CAN. Society has taught us that when we find ourselves at ground zero, we have to immediately pull ourselves up by the bootstraps and start searching for the silver lining. But I'm here to tell you: It doesn't have to be that way. Life is hard, and we can let it be. We have to let it be. It's the only way to reach a place of acceptance with our new situation, our new set of circumstances, our new LIFE.

Your life will be different, but it will be amazing.

Kevin took his first step a few days after receiving that precious note from Livi, and we cheered. And watching him be so brave made me brave enough to take my first step toward my new life, too.

A few weeks after his accident, I left my publisher and never looked back. And though I didn't know what was ahead for me, I knew I was ready for it. And more than that, I knew I was ENOUGH for it. And for whatever else would come my way.

And so are you.

You Are Enough

Your life WILL be different. Whatever you lost—a person, a love, a job, a limb, a dream, your way—it will be different. There's no minimizing that. But accepting that there's no minimizing it and choosing to keep putting one foot in front of the other anyway...THAT'S when the amazing part is going to kick in. Realizing that the worst has happened, or at least the very bad has happened, and you SURVIVED. You survived and you felt and you lived it, and you didn't run from it or try to turn it into some glittery aha moment. YOU ENDURED AND YOU PREVAILED. You were enough to handle every single thing that came your way.

God never promised we wouldn't know pain. He isn't the author of it, but He isn't the bodyguard blocking it from us either. Jesus Himself knew intense, agonizing pain. The worst kind, as a matter of fact. Betrayal. False accusations. A humiliating death on a cross for a crime He didn't commit. No, God never promised us we wouldn't know pain. That we wouldn't know ground-zero moments and dark nights of the soul. What He

DID promise was to be with us in the midst of our pain. To help shoulder our burdens. To bring beauty from the ashes. To help us accept the different so we can get to the amazing.

chapter 4

LOOKING FOR LOVE

*M*y family had faced down big, hard, life-altering things, and we were still standing. And I was without a publisher for the first time in years. Everything in my life felt new and uncertain and stripped-down. No publisher, no pretense, no book deal: I was back to the days of just me, my laptop, and an open heart. And I was longing for a new direction for my life. I wanted what had seemed to elude me thus far at age thirty-seven— I wanted the family. The husband. The dream. The 2.5 kids and the picket fence and the whole nine. Who can't relate to that? I decided it was time to take action toward that dream.

In hindsight, I can look back now and see how raw

and vulnerable I was during that season. How the tragedy that had befallen my family had reminded me just how scary and heartbreaking and harsh life can be, and how I was searching for some kind of guarantee or insurance policy to help buffer that reality. Not that it wasn't a perfectly normal and healthy desire: to date and fall in love and get married. Particularly given the fact that I had been in the throes of a self-imposed dating hiatus since my last devastating heartbreak two years earlier. But choosing to embark upon my search for love when so many other things in my life were changing at that moment probably wasn't the wisest decision. When you're still reeling from any sort of life-altering event, it's best to take a pause and let the waters calm a little before adding any other waves of change to the mix. Things were already so precarious and shaky in my life that I wasn't emotionally equipped to deal with any further upheaval. And what is a relationship, if not a complete and total upheaval to everything your life has been before that relationship came along?

In that moment, though, I couldn't see any of that. I wanted to LIVE. I wanted to experience life and love to the fullest, regardless of the consequences. Having seen firsthand how fragile life could be, I was determined to completely drop the walls I had so carefully erected around my heart for the past two years and be completely open to whoever and whatever came my way. I decided I would try a dating app, since so many people I knew seemed to be using them . . . and even having luck!

Bumble was my app of choice, and I was pleasantly surprised to see how many quality, attractive, successful men were out there. Men I almost certainly wouldn't cross paths with outside of that little app.

I want to take a second now and address the whole online dating debate. I've heard all the critics and the negative Nancys saying everything from "It will make me look desperate" to "There are no good men on there" to "If you really trusted God, you wouldn't have to rely on a dating app." And I'd like to just say, STOP WITH THE NAY-SAYING. Online dating and dating apps may not be for you, and that's okay, but that doesn't mean they're not right for other people. I know couples who are in happy relationships and marriages who met online or on a dating app. This is simply the technology-driven, fast-paced modern world we live in.

For people like me, who don't want to hang out at bars and clubs, who work from home, and who feel like they're more likely to encounter a glitter-breathing unicorn than they are a single man under the age of fifty at church, there are few viable options for meeting someone. Sure, there are some sketchy dudes on dating apps, but there are sketchy dudes everywhere. There are also some really great guys on there. You just have to have patience, a positive attitude, and an open mind. And don't even get me started on the idea that you don't trust God if you use a dating app. God changed not just my entire career path but my entire LIFE through social media and technology, so who's to say He can't bring me my person via Bumble? I mean, you wouldn't even be reading this book right now if it weren't for the power of Twitter (that's where I was first "discovered" and approached by a publisher about writing my first book), so I'm not going to limit God like that. If He can turn water into wine, he can certainly turn an online date into a soul mate!

Okay . . . stepping off my soapbox now.

Maybe that moment in my life wasn't the ideal time to be vulnerable and put myself out there, but it made me feel alive. I had an active dating life for the first time in years! Granted, a couple of the dates rated somewhere up there with getting my fingernails plucked out one by one, but it still felt good being bold and taking risks and being an active participant in my love life, instead of just sitting on the sidelines like I had been doing for the past two years.

And, also in hindsight, I don't think I would change a thing about the decision to put myself out there again. Because if I did, if I changed even one tiny little thing about that season, I wouldn't be where I am today. I wouldn't be WHO I am today. I wouldn't have fought the hardest battles of my life and won. I wouldn't have experienced the lows that come with looking for love, but neither would I have experienced the highs. I wouldn't have found closure with a decade-long relationship or found the best friend of my life or even be writing this book right now.

No, I wouldn't have experienced the heartbreak that was coming.

But neither would I have experienced the healing and becoming whole that would follow.

And I might have never grasped the simple truth that I am enough. I am enough for a dating app. I am enough for any man I might find on that dating app (whether he realizes it or not). I am enough, and deserving and worthy of love and laughter and the very best life has to offer.

And so are you.

So I urge you to put yourself out there. Be vulnerable. Take a chance. Step outside your comfort zone. Try something new and daring and audacious. Maybe it's getting on Bumble (or another dating app). Maybe it's changing jobs or changing cities or simply changing your hair color. But do something different from what you do every single day. Take a risk. Even if you're not ready to. Because you never know how important and vital the sentence you're writing today is to the bigger story your life is trying to tell.

You Are Enough

In previous books and writings of mine, I've said things along the lines of Why settle for a happy ending instead of holding out for a happy everything? *But life and loss and experience have taught me that there's no such thing as a happy EVERYTHING. And you know what? That's okay. Because the beauty of life is in its shades of light and dark, heart-break and healing, joy and sadness, laughter and tears. Everything can't possibly be happy, because then NOTHING would be happy. Instead of looking for the happy ending OR the happy everything, how about we just look for the happy RIGHT NOW? The glimmers of magic in the mundane. The simple joys that make life so sweet. How about we just live the stuffing out of life and welcome everything that shows up—the good and the bad—knowing it's all a part of our story? And knowing that IT IS ENOUGH? It's an audacious way to live, indeed, standing with the door to your heart and life wide-open. But isn't that the REAL fairy tale...a brave, bold, well-lived life?*

chapter 5

IN TWENTY-FIVE DAYS

*I*f I could have a conversation with Fall 2016 Mandy:

In twenty-five days, you're going to meet him. And it's going to change your life. Not because he's going to be a great love of your life...but because he's going to remind you that the possibility of great love is still out there. He's going to open you up and make you reach for more. He's going to remind you how to be vulnerable with another human being. He's going to leap right over every wall you spent years crafting and perfecting.

He's going to make you smile and laugh and feel, and remind you what it's like to not be alone. That's a powerful feeling—the feeling of not being alone. You haven't felt it in more than two years. There's a sense of enoughness that comes with not feeling alone, a sense of okayness. A sense of *Whew. I can exhale now. Everything is right with the world.*

And then, just as you start to relax into him a little bit, he's going to leave. And it's going to hurt. And when he goes, your very fragile sense of enoughness will go right out the door with him. Because his departure is going to bring up the whirling, swirling hurricane of emotions that descended upon you when the one before him, the one you loved for all those years, left. The one who inspired you to erect all those walls around your heart in the first place. And all of this is going to create a perfect storm in your life that will force you to confront all the struggles and sorrows and fears and frustrations you've been holding at bay for so long. You see, you haven't yet learned that your worth isn't found in him. Or in the man before him. Or in any man at all. You are still fighting for your worth and looking for it in all the wrong places. Sometimes it takes being left seemingly with nothing to realize that you are everything. To see that you held the key to your own happiness and self-worth and belonging and wholeness all along.

Over the course of the next year, you will fight the hardest battle of your life as you wrestle with all the old ghosts: Fear of abandonment. Fear of being alone. Fear of being broken beyond repair. Fear of being unlovable, and unwanted, and unworthy. Fear of being simply *not enough*. And through this process, you will become a different person. You will become a person who knows herself. Who accepts herself. And who loves herself, just as she is, regardless of who else does or doesn't choose to stay in her life.

It will take time and tears, and fighting and scraping your way out of the depths of despair, but you will get there. And on the other side, you will be stronger and braver and better for it. Because you will now be someone who really does love herself, instead of just someone who knows how to craft shiny, clever sentences that make it sound like you do. You will be someone who knows she's enough for anyone... even the ones who don't stick around. You will be someone who knows that sometimes it takes great heartbreak to bring about even greater healing and wholeness.

That other version of you is waiting on the other side of all of this. She's waiting for you. Don't lose sight of her. Don't get so caught up in the big loss that you miss the bigger lesson.

Yes, Mandy, in twenty-five days, you're going to meet him. And it's going to change your life.

It probably won't change his. He'll probably never know the impact he had on your life at all, unless he finds his way to this book. You were merely a sentence in his story while he was several chapters in yours. And that's okay. Because some people come into our lives not to be loved, but to be lost and learned from in order to help us change and grow. That was always their purpose. To try and assign them a different one would be as futile as trying to stop time.

27

So many people bump into our lives for a second, and it changes us forever but they never know it. And while that's funny and strange and a little sad, it's also just life. And the truth of the matter is, it was never really about them anyway. It was always about us and what we were meant to learn from them. It was always about us and who we were meant to BECOME as a result of having encountered them.

So, Fall 2016 Mandy... in twenty-five days, you're going to meet him. And while part of me wants to tell you to turn and run in the opposite direction, a much bigger part knows I wouldn't be Today Mandy if you did. So go. Go forth with your arms and heart as wide-open as you did back then. And I'll see you on the other side.

You Are Enough

No matter what happened. No matter how it ended. No matter how many tears were cried or doors were pounded on but never opened. No matter how many bruises were formed from knees hitting the floor as you said prayers that seemed to go unanswered. (They didn't ACTUALLY go unanswered...It just takes growth and maturity and wisdom to realize that sometimes no is the most loving, gentle answer God can give.) No matter how badly they hurt you when they walked away. No matter how many times you let them come closer when you should have said, "Stay away." No matter how many times you took the same dead-end road. No matter how many times you said yes when you really meant no. No matter how many regrets are now blowing in the wind. No matter how many text messages you should have deleted instead of hit "Send." No matter who, what, where, when, how, or why. No matter. No matter. NO MATTER.

You. Are. Enough.

chapter 6

THE BOY UPSTAIRS

I heard my upstairs neighbor for a year before I met him.

Walking around above me, playing music, watching *How I Met Your Mother* and *Parks and Recreation*. I often thought two things to myself: (1) *Wow, these walls are thin!* and (2) *He watches two of my favorite shows all the time, so we would probably be BFFs.* I admit, I wondered about him at times, this mysterious Netflix-loving neighbor of mine. But I never in a million years thought I would wind up dating him.

Until Bumble came into my life.

Yes, after a self-imposed two-year hiatus from dating, I had decided it was time to get back out there again.

And after a few first dates that didn't go anywhere...a guy popped into my "match queue" who was listed as .4 miles away (Bumble is a location-based dating app). *Wow,* I thought. *This guy is practically in my backyard!*

Little did I know that this guy was *literally* in my backyard.

He knew who I was; I had no clue who he was. Apparently, we had said hi in the parking lot a few times over the course of the past year, but I had no recollection of it. When I met him in person for the first time, I was struck by how cute he was. And especially by how blue his eyes were. How had I managed to miss THIS guy in the parking lot for an entire year?! (Sometimes I think I must be the most oblivious person on earth.)

Anyway...from pretty early on, I felt a connection with him. I was attracted to him, of course, but beyond that, I found him funny, witty, smart, and entirely unique. His ability to banter especially impressed me. Nothing is more attractive to me than a man who can banter. Throw in a side of sarcastic humor and you've REALLY got my attention. This guy had both. And I liked him, which was new for me. "Like" can be very hard to come by in my world. It just doesn't happen very often for me.

We hung out a lot over that first month...took walks, played Scrabble, watched movies. And for the first time in years, I could feel my guard start to slowly come down. The guard that had been firmly in place for two years, ever since my heart was smashed into a million pieces by the last man I cared for (i.e., Mr. E from my previous books). And, honestly, I'd been pretty closed off for years before that. I had spent the greater part of seven years feeling like I was never quite "enough" for the man I loved more than anything to love me back. Never feeling loved or valued or desired by him had closed me off completely.

Until The Boy Upstairs (a.k.a. TBU) came along.

He was broken. He'd be the first one to tell you that. Not even a year out of a heartbreaking divorce, he was gun-shy. Emotionally guarded. Fearful of taking a chance on someone who might turn around and hurt him like he'd been hurt before. I was coming from a pretty broken place myself, so suffice it to say that between the two of us, we had some serious baggage. I'd been keeping people at bay from a place of fear while he'd been serial dating from a place of pain. I guess it didn't exactly make for a perfect combination.

But in spite of that, or maybe even BECAUSE of that, there was a connection there. I liked him. I knew he liked me. I was comfortable with him. Didn't worry about how "perfect" I looked around him. I could just be myself. My equally broken, baggage-laden, messy self. It was really nice.

Until it wasn't.

A month or so in, things started to crumble. A pebble or two at a time...then a rock or two at a time. Then it collapsed completely. And I was left standing there in the rubble feeling confused about what had just happened. I had finally met a man that I liked. A man who made me want to drop my walls a little. A man who made me laugh. And he was gone. Except not really gone, because he lived right above me, and the walls were so thin I could hear him sneeze.

What I had with TBU wasn't really even a "relationship," and I don't know that it ever would have been. He was terrified of commitment; I was less than two months into my return to the dating scene and far from ready for one. I didn't know what the future held. But I sure enjoyed the present. For once, it was enough for me. Just spending time with him, talking and laughing and watching Netflix and having him teach me all about geocaching, was enough for me.

If you've never heard of it, geocaching is defined as "a real-world, outdoor treasure hunting game using GPS-enabled devices. Participants navigate to a specific set of GPS coordinates and then attempt to find the geocache (container) hidden at that location." Basically there are geocaches hidden everywhere around the world, probably some in your own town right this minute. The cool thing is, they're hidden in the most ordinary places: Hanging from a tree in a parking lot. On the side of a stop sign. Behind books on a library shelf. But if you don't have eyes to see them, you won't. They're so subtly hidden in plain sight, it can be easy to overlook the very thing you're looking for.

Much like my neighbor. The guy hidden in plain sight who would one day open me up to the idea of dating again for the first time in a while.

34

And much like my process of healing and becoming whole, which was hidden behind the heartbreak I would experience by taking my first shot at finding love in two years and coming up short.

I was happy TBU was the one who reintroduced me to the dating world. It was kinda perfect, really, that someone so close to home, literally one wall away from me, inspired me to drop my walls.

But it was also messy and painful and even scary to have those walls dropped and to be left standing there, vulnerable and alone. Alone just like I was two years before, when Mr. E sat me down, looked me in the face, and told me he didn't love me.

All the old feelings of rejection and self-doubt and insecurity started to creep in. I began to ask myself the same old painful questions I had been asking myself for years now: *Why wasn't I enough for him? Why am I never enough for anyone? What's wrong with me?* The Boy Upstairs wasn't the cause of it all, but he was definitely the catalyst. The tipping point—of unresolved heartache from two years earlier, my family tragedy, and uncertainty about my career path and my future as a writer—had been reached. Putting myself out there emotionally even in a small way, to be almost immediately rejected again, left me feeling raw and small and heartsick.

I couldn't see what was happening then, as I was too close to it all. Too in the thick of things. I was slowly, piece by piece, losing myself. My sense of control. My publishing deal. A relationship that had signified to me my ability to move on and try again after incredible heartache.

Yes, I was losing myself.

But I was also finding myself.

Sometimes the finding is in the losing, as I would soon find out.

You Are Enough

If you feel like they took your self-worth with them when they left...they didn't.

If life has hurt you so badly you feel like you might never be whole again...you will.

If the end of the relationship or the job or the opportunity feels like the end of every-thing that matters...it isn't.

It's actually just the beginning.

chapter 7

LOSING MYSELF

What followed were dark days.

I felt myself start to shut down, little by little. Disappointment—in love, in career, in LIFE—was weighing me down. So much so that I began to withdraw from everything and everyone. I looked around at our world. The dissension and anger and violence and hatred I saw on the news and on social media only served to deepen my disillusionment and melancholy.

I felt aimless and lost. Confused. I couldn't seem to find the words to write anymore. I felt so exposed and vulnerable in my personal life that it bled into my professional life. The way I saw it, I had finally been brave enough to put myself out there again and I had been almost immediately rejected by the first guy I allowed myself to have feelings for.

Mind you, this growing feeling of hopelessness wasn't all based on a month-long relationship that went wrong. That's not how depression works. It builds up, slowly and sneakily, one disappointment at a time, and chips away at your spirit, a little at a time. It's like the lights slowly dimming in a restaurant. You don't even realize it's happening until you look up and it's much darker and you find yourself searching for the smallest speck of light. Supposedly in a restaurant, the dimming of lights is designed to heighten your sense of taste. In real life, however, the dimming of light dulls your senses. Leaves you numb, and apathetic, and empty. And that's what my life was slowly but surely becoming. Numb, apathetic, and empty.

You never know what the final straw is going to be that pushes you from teetering on the edge of depression to full-blown depression. I had battled clinical depression in my mid-twenties, which I've written about at length, and fought my way back successfully to a place of well-being and emotional stability. I went through another, much less severe bout of depression a few years ago that I documented in my book *Beautiful Uncertainty*.

What I can see now, looking back, is that I never quite healed from that second run-in. Having the man I had loved for almost a decade (Mr. E) look me in the eyes and tell me with little emotion that he didn't love me, didn't want to be with me, and was no longer even attracted to me was hugely emotionally damaging. More so than I even realized at the time. I can remember barely crying after he left my house that day. It was like I shut myself down completely and never allowed myself to contend with the fallout of his rejection.

And yet, back in 2014, almost exactly six months to the day that he delivered his emotional blow, I started having severe heart palpitations completely and totally out of the blue. The doctors ran every test imaginable. I wore a heart monitor. I saw a cardiologist. And every last physical ailment was ruled out. Meaning the heart palpitations were happening as a result of overwhelming emotions I wasn't ready for or prepared to deal with at the time. Or, as my therapist said just the other day when we were discussing it, my heart was, quite literally, broken. And instead of dealing with it and facing the grief head-on, I was attempting to do my usual pull-myself-up-by-the-bootstraps act and find the silver lining of my sadness and move on with my head held high, like the confident woman I projected to the world.

Only I wasn't that woman anymore. I wasn't sure who I was.

Couple all that with my brother-in-law's near-fatal accident and the strain on my family, leaving my publisher of four years and facing career uncertainty, and now dealing with yet another romantic disappointment, and I was just flattened. Spent. I had nothing left in my emotional reserves. I felt depleted and defeated. And I felt completely and overwhelmingly inadequate. Like I was hopelessly broken and flawed. I was not enough for my ex, not enough for The Boy Upstairs, not enough for my publisher or my friends or my readers, or anyone at all.

I felt like nothing. Like a waste of space. As I imagine you might have felt before and might be feeling right this moment, as you read this.

I'd like to be able to tell you some quick and easy fix for how I swiftly kicked my depression's butt and reclaimed my life again, but it didn't work that way this time. This time, I was doubting everything about myself. This time, the depression was all-consuming and encompassing every aspect of my life. Even physically, I couldn't escape the reality that I wasn't enough. Why? Because The Boy Upstairs was still living right above me, a constant reminder of my latest failed relationship. I could hear him up there, living his life, moving on with things, having girls over...while I idled away downstairs, asking myself the same questions over and over: *Why was I not enough? Why am I never enough?*

As many of you in your thirties and beyond who are still single can attest to, after a while, after a certain number of relationships crash and burn, you just start to feel like you're inherently flawed and destined for a life alone. You look around and on Facebook and see the images of happy couples and families, and you feel like you will always be on the outside, looking in. You start to question why finding love is so easy for them and so hard for you. And all the inspirational quotes and self-help books and pep talks from your girlfriends don't seem to fill that empty void created by the love you want so badly that somehow keeps eluding you.

The Bible says, "Unrelenting disappointment leaves you heartsick, but a sudden good break can turn life around" (Prov. 13:12 MSG). I was facing one unrelenting disappointment after another in the fall of 2016, and my heart was most definitely sick. But one might argue that the "sudden good break" had already happened. What if the heartbreak I was experiencing as a result of my failed romance with The Boy Upstairs was my "sudden good break"? What if I needed to experience that break to fully deal with the one that came before? What if, as the man on the street had predicted months earlier, I was, in fact, losing myself to find myself?

And what if I needed to get down to absolutely nothing to realize that I was *everything?*

Dorothy Gale of Kansas had the power all along. She just had to learn it for herself, Glinda the Good Witch told her in the classic move *The Wizard of Oz.*

A tornado was raging through my life, and the light was growing dimmer by the minute.

But I would soon discover that, all along, the power was within me.

Just as it is in you.

You Are Enough

I hope you remember that no matter what this moment holds...the next one could hold something beautiful and magical and astonishing. So hold on. Hold on and know that even though pain may be taking your breath away today, it could be beauty that takes your breath away tomorrow. Life is funny like that. And sadness never, ever, EVER gets the last word.

That job and that relationship and that opportunity you didn't get...oh man, will it ever feel in the moment like you missed out on something.

But later...maybe even years later...you will come to see that this great thing that you thought you lost was really a great big bullet that you dodged.

And then you will say a silent prayer of gratitude for that "almost" that never became a "definitely."

That stop sign that never became a green light.

That no that never became a yes.

chapter 8

WHY I'M STILL SINGLE
(THE UGLY TRUTH)

Why do I SAY I'm still single?

A pithy "Because I'm too fabulous to settle."

A polite "Because I'm waiting for God to bring me the right man."

A peppy "Because there are still things I'm meant to accomplish as a single woman!"

But the truth is... during the dark nights of my soul, I think the reason I'm still single is because I'm inherently flawed.

Bad. Ugly. Undeserving. Screwed-up. Unlovable.

THIS is the underbelly of singleness. The dark side. Where the rubber meets the road. Where the truth comes out. And it's not the slightest bit pretty, or inspirational, or even positive.

It is, in fact, very ugly.

Because of its ugliness, it's also a truth I have kept to myself. I've dressed it up in pretty pink girl power with a silver lining, instead of getting really, really REAL with myself about my fears about being single and thirty-nine. And in doing that, my friends and readers, I feel I have, at times, done you a disservice. I have done myself a disservice. It has been called to my attention recently that I have been known to use positivity as a defense mechanism. Oh, I was angry when I heard that. Fearful. Indignant. Convinced the person telling me that HAD to be mistaken. "I'm just a positive person!" I argued. If I don't look for the silver lining...what is the purpose to the bad things that happen? If I choose to let in the darkness and the sadness and the REALNESS...won't I sink in it? Won't it drown me? Won't it make me a...SHUDDER...negative person?!

The truth is, I don't know exactly why I'm still single. I think I'm starting to come to a better understanding of why, but for the moment, it's still just shadowed and blurry truth that I'm struggling to make sense of. But the reasons I've often convinced myself about why I'm still single aren't pretty.

I rarely meet guys. Organically, anyway. Like...literally NEVER. A few years ago, I felt like I could simply walk into a room and command the attention of the men there. I had no trouble meeting men. I even got hit on regularly. But something changed along the way, and that's not my experience anymore. I suspect it was more an internal change than an external one, as I am honestly more confident in my physical appearance now than I was ten years ago. The toxic relationship in my late twenties that inspired the creation of my blog but left me questioning everything about myself took its toll. Life happened. The man I loved for almost ten years sat in my apartment and told me in no uncertain terms that I wasn't lovable to him. That I was flawed. That he had abruptly stopped being attracted to me, after almost a decade of intense, undeniable chemistry. That my humanity and my imperfections were a turnoff to him. He had confirmed all my worst fears about myself: that simply being ME wasn't enough.

I can't blame all of my self-doubts on men, though. That's too easy. That's a refusal to take responsibility for my own life and choices and attitudes and self-image, and I won't do that. I will hand them their share of the blame, but I'll take my share, too. The negative self-talk? Yep, I'm a pro.

You're too ugly.

You're too fat.

You have a gap in your teeth.

You look old.

You've done too many bad things in your life, and you don't deserve to ever find love.

God has forgotten you.

It's so easy for everyone else and so difficult for you.

You're meant to wander the earth alone forever.

You will always be on the outside, looking in.

And on and on and on, like a broken record.

"You just need more makeup, a thigh gap, more self-love!" the secular world says superficially.

"You just need more faith," the Christian world says judgmentally.

I have faith. Lots of faith. Even though my faith in Christianity has sometimes wavered, I always find my way back to the core truth that I love Jesus with my whole heart.

I also have makeup, lots of makeup, and I'm working on the self-love stuff every day. (But I don't—and doubt I will ever—have a thigh gap. Just not in the cards for me.)

I want with every single fiber of my being to be one of those self-assured, confident, bold women of God who knows exactly who she is, and walks in the freedom of knowing how loved she is, how precious she is, how validated she is.

I want to be that woman, but I'm not that woman yet. I'm on a journey to become her. And that journey starts with this book and these moments of honesty that will hopefully be followed by lots more moments of honesty as I stop frantically searching for the silver lining of every situation and instead just learn to embrace the ugliness, the doubt, the uncertainty, the fear...as all a part of the journey. This is it, ladies. These are the trenches of single life. And that's not to say we should walk around like Eeyore all the time, feeling sorry for ourselves and playing the victim of our lives. Not at all. But neither should we bounce around like Tigger all the time...springing when we feel like sighing. Laughing when we feel like crying. And running from our truth by lying.

Part of being the heroine of your own life is accepting the bad with the good. Not dodging it or covering it up or glossing over it to make it look prettier and more pleasing so you can prop it up in the corner and not have to deal with it. I personally think it's a lot braver to talk about your doubts and fears instead of acting like everything's perfect. And life without both joy AND sadness is a life without balance.

The truth is...single life is hard. It's HARD. It lends itself to loneliness and self-doubt and fear.

Life in general is hard. Bad things happen. People leave. Things change. Disappointment is inevitable.

But I think it's high time to march all of that loneliness and self-doubt and fear and rejection and disappointment and depression and anxiety into the light, to stop hiding it all away and acting like it doesn't exist, because to admit that it DOES exist is to admit vulnerability. And to give everything a more positive sheen in order to make ourselves feel better for the moment actually only harms us more in the long run. (Believe me, I am living proof of this fact.)

So let's just be who we are and be really, really okay with it...shall we? Single and uncertain. Messy but magical. Sometimes lonely but oh so worthy of love, especially our own. And here's something revolutionary I want you to consider: Perhaps you're still single because that's simply the way the cookie has crumbled so far. Not because of how flawed or how imperfect you are. And not because of any secret, terrible fear you might have about yourself. Whatever your fears are about yourself, you're not alone. YOU ARE NOT ALONE. We all have fears about ourselves. Married people have fears about themselves the same as us single folks do.

So whatever ways you've managed to convince yourself that you're not enough—for love, for dating, for a man, for marriage—throw them out the window! YOU ARE ENOUGH. Regardless of your relationship status and the lies you tell yourself about it. Regardless of what has happened to you in life. Regardless of how many "cons" you can rattle off on your own pros-and-cons list. You might have a million and one "ugly truths" about yourself to list there, but none of them negate the fact that you are real and authentic and human, and that means you're going to sometimes be a mess and make a mess and feel like a mess. And that's okay. Because every single day, you get closer to becoming the woman you're meant to be, and there's absolutely nothing in this world more beautiful than that.

You Are Enough

See her there? That girl with the big smile and the even bigger confidence and the bounce in her step? That girl who loves her-

self and has no time for nonsense and likes drama only on her television and not in her life? She's so strong and so blissfully self-approved, and so immune to anything and anyone who tries to bring her down. She only chases goals and dreams, and never people or their affection. She's all aglow with the knowledge of all she is worthy of, and "settling" isn't even a word in her vocabulary. See her there, shining without apology?

That's you. The YOU that's waiting around the corner of everything you're going through right now.

You see, only people who've been through the fire can possess that light within. Only people who have been knocked down can have the strength and courage to try again. Only people who have been told they CAN'T are gritty enough to knock off that T and show the world they can.

And only women who have been hurt by love and carry on anyway know their value is not determined by a man.

She's there, waiting for you, on the other side of your heartbreak and fear and self-doubt.

Don't give up on her.

chapter 9

ROCK BOTTOM

*T*he twisted sisters of depression and anxiety had moved back into my life.

Ironically, they moved in just as I moved out, from under The Boy Upstairs into an apartment two doors down instead. I had the idea that if I couldn't hear his every move and be constantly reminded of his existence and the crash-and-burn nature of our "almost relationship," I might be able to move on with my life faster. A fresh start was all I needed, right?

But it wasn't that simple, of course. I was still treating the symptom and not the root cause of my depression. I was still under the mistaken impression that I was just "sad" about yet another relationship biting the dust, when in reality, the issues I was struggling with had been festering for years and were much bigger than that. Yes, I was sad about TBU deciding he didn't want to date me anymore, but what the ending of that relationship triggered in me was something much deeper and darker. That relationship became symbolic for every relationship failure I had ever experienced. I started replaying every rejection, romantic or otherwise, that I had ever experienced in my life. And I allowed those rejections to play on a loop in my mind constantly. My mental refrain became *I'm not enough. I'm never going to be enough. People don't want me around. I don't matter. My whole life is going to be like this, always on the outside, looking in. I'm going to die alone. I can't live like this anymore.*

Depression lies to you. It tells you all the things I was telling myself and more. Let me clarify this fact right now: "Depression" is NOT synonymous with "sadness." It's not something you can just "get over." It's not a matter of not praying enough or not trusting God enough or not being grateful enough. Believe me, I've heard all of those things and more from well-meaning family members and friends. When you allow yourself to believe the falsity that depression is something you should be able to just brush off, you set yourself up to feel like even more of a failure when you're not able to brush it off.

Which I, of course, did. I couldn't understand why I was letting one guy and the ending of one relationship take me under the way that it was. But it wasn't about the one guy or the one relationship. It was about the chemicals in my brain not functioning properly. It was about long-term and deep-seated emotional trauma I hadn't properly dealt with. And it would take more than a new apartment or a new haircut or a night out with my girlfriends to fix it.

The world we are living in is messy, complicated, and, at times, frightening. Anxiety and depression are at an all-time high. According to the Centers for Disease Control and Prevention, suicide is the tenth leading cause of death in the United States. Eight hundred thousand people around the world die due to suicide every year, according to the World Health Organization. That's one person every forty seconds. Very few people, particularly if you're in the Christian community, like me, are talking frankly about these alarming stats and mental health issues and how to address them in a real, clinical way. I certainly believe that people can be healed of any and all diseases in miraculous ways, but you shouldn't feel like you're doing something wrong if you're not able to "pray your depression away." You need HELP. Medical attention and emotional support. And there's nothing wrong with asking for that help.

My cry for help came one day in early December 2016, not long after I had moved into my new apartment. There was a cloud of darkness hanging over that apartment that was almost palpable, so much so that friends of mine who would come over to visit noticed it. I hadn't even bothered to decorate for Christmas, because I felt so overwhelmed by the move and trying to get my apartment organized and just life in general. Being a complete and total Christmas freak, that was a big deal for me.

And the day came when I didn't even have the energy or desire to get out of bed at all. I simply decided I had had enough, and I was throwing in the towel. The constant refrain in my head of *You are not enough* was deafening and exhausting. I turned a fan and a white-noise machine on high to drown out all sound, I got into my bed and pulled the covers over my head, and I shut off my phone. I was done. I couldn't go one step further.

Was I suicidal? People have asked me. Not to the degree of making a plan and actually taking action to hurt myself, no. But I was definitely struggling with thoughts like *I'm a major burden to everyone in my life, and I can't go on like this.* When you're stuck in a loop of severe clinical depression, you can't see a day when you WON'T feel miserable. You can't see the light at the end of the tunnel. Or if you can, you don't have the energy to try to claw your way toward that light, because the darkness is simply too overwhelming.

I'm lucky in a way that many people aren't. I have a family that refused to leave me stuck in the hellish purgatory my life had become. My parents tried to call me over and over that day, and when I didn't answer, my dad came to my apartment. He banged and banged on the door until I finally heard him over the noise of the fan and the sound machine.

And then he sat me down and told me we had to make a plan. We had to seek professional help.

So we did.

We went to a nearby mental health facility, where I had gone through an intensive outpatient program, or IOP, a couple of years prior for the anxiety-based heart palpitations I was having. It proved to be very helpful for me the first time around, so they recommended I enroll in IOP once again.

I started IOP the next day and attended faithfully, three times a week, three hours per session. For those of you who aren't familiar with IOP, it's essentially group therapy. You're in a room with anywhere from five to twenty people who are going through similar things as you, and you talk about your problems and receive both group feedback and therapist feedback. In addition, there are often daily lessons taught that touch on various coping skills. Though I had never heard of group therapy before my first experience with it in 2014, I was a big believer in all kinds of therapy and had seen firsthand the difference the group format made in my ability to navigate my anxiety.

This time around, however, things were different.

I found little relief in the IOP program. My depression continued to worsen. I could barely force myself out of bed. My quality of life continued to deteriorate. So that's how my dad and I found ourselves, the day after Christmas, back at the facility, begging for a better solution.

The next recommended step was something called partial hospitalization, or PHP. I had never heard of this, and the idea of actually being hospitalized was frightening to me. But the counselor at the facility was very reassuring and explained to me that "partial hospitalization" simply meant I would be at the hospital every day, undergoing intensive group therapy from nine o'clock to two thirty. I would have to surrender my phone when I arrived each morning, but I would go home each afternoon and not have to stay at the hospital overnight. It was more of an immersive experience than IOP and would also allow me to meet regularly with a psychiatrist one-on-one to discuss the medicinal side of treatment.

We had a plan. The counselor started to enroll me at a location in Nashville, since the facility I was attending for IOP didn't offer a PHP program, but at the last minute, she changed it to a facility about half an hour away, in Franklin. We'll call it Whispering Pines. I had no idea, at that moment, that her split-second decision to place me at Whispering Pines would change my life. That I was about to meet people who would make me feel worthwhile again. And that there I would come to find not just a sense of belonging for perhaps the first time in my life...but healing and wholeness as well.

You Are Enough

Mental health is still, sadly, such a misunderstood thing. Most people struggle with it to some degree at least once in their lives, or have their lives impacted by it in some way or another, whether it's through a friend or family member...yet there's still so much shame attached to it. We feel like we have to "man up" or "woman up" and carry on with things like we haven't a care in the world when, really, we are suffering deeply. Anxiety and depression have been those ever-present shadows in my life that I can't seem to outrun no matter how hard I try. What people without mental health issues don't understand is that the smallest things, normal things, tiny molehills...can turn into great big gigantic mountains when you're weighted down by anxiety and depression. So what I know standing where I do now is this: If you have a mental illness of any kind, good grief are you brave for simply getting up every day and continuing to put one foot in front of the other! Please know that you don't have to hide your struggles—but neither do you have to be defined by them. You are a whole, complete person made up of many beautiful parts and many broken parts—but neither determine the course of your life. You do, and God does. You are enough, just as you are. And you're really, really brave for taking steps to be even better.

chapter 10

WHISKEY AND ZOLOFT

*D*uring my battle with depression in the winter of 2016, I tried to talk to other people who had been through similar struggles as often as I could, simply because it helped me not to feel so alone on my own path of heartbreak and healing. For days after talking with a friend who had recently endured a painful and life-altering divorce, something he shared with me struck me so powerfully I couldn't stop thinking about it. He said that during the awful, heart-wrenching time right after his divorce, he was held together by whiskey and Zoloft. Not by friends or family or his church or even God Himself. What kept him going was whiskey and Zoloft. And as a person of faith, it surprised me how much I could relate to the *Where was God in all this?* sentiment.

Why would I relate so much to that feeling? Perhaps because during my big life crash in 2016, I felt abandoned by people . . . and, yes, even a little abandoned by God. Why does it feel so scary to type those words? I mean, the Israelites felt abandoned by God. David regularly felt abandoned by God. Jesus Himself even felt abandoned by God on the cross! So why is it so uncomfortable for me to see it written in black and white that *I* have? Why is it hard for me to acknowledge that there have been times in my life when I fell apart only to be put back together by things other than God?

There was the time after a bad breakup that I was held together by the show *Lost*. This was before Netflix, so I drove to Blockbuster every other day to rent the next season. It was the only thing that got me through. There was my massive life crash in my mid-twenties when I was held together by therapy and antidepressants and antianxiety meds. There've been times when I've been held together by friends, by food, by family, by self-help books. Even my writing has often been my saving grace.

And, yes, there have also been times when the only thing that gathered the pieces of my life and heart back together was God. Particularly the season my family and I went through right after my brother-in-law's accident. I could tell you story after story of God's divine grace that fell on my family during that time. It was a bittersweet season of great loss met with great compassion and love and mercy. Every day, I'm filled with massive gratitude that although the accident took Kevin's leg, God spared Kevin's life.

But that hasn't always been the case for me. I haven't always felt God's hand or intervention during seasons of struggle. And I'm guessing that might feel true for a lot of you, too. And it's okay to admit that.

During my struggles in 2016, it wasn't God who initially put me back together. It was my family. It was the new-found band of brothers and sisters I found at Whispering Pines. It was my therapists. It was a new antidepressant. And, yes, you can argue that God led me to all those things, and I won't deny that. But in the immediacy of the moment, in the darkest nights of my soul, I didn't feel Him. He seemed to be hiding, just out of sight.

God doesn't always spare the marriage. Or the leg. Or the life. I can't answer why. There are endless things about God that I don't understand and may never understand this side of heaven. But what I do know with great certainty is that sometimes, when God feels like He's a million miles away, survival is simply about whatever gets you through the day. Sometimes you just have to patch yourself back up with whatever tools you have at your disposal in that moment.

I'm probably going to get pushback on this. Some of you may be feeling all sorts of ways as you read this. And that's okay. I'm not afraid to admit to the world that I have some questions for God. That sometimes I haven't sensed His presence or understood His people or trusted

His power. That I get frustrated that He doesn't talk to me audibly when I really need answers. That I have been known to turn to other things and people to glue me back together when His hands feel far removed from me.

There's a rather cliché quote that says something along the lines of "If God feels far away from you, guess who moved?" I find this quote to be extremely patronizing and judgy. Who was ever comforted or uplifted by that quote? You're already feeling distant from God, and then someone comes along and instead of offering words of encouragement or understanding, they tell you it's your fault that you feel distant from God. And maybe it is.

But then again, maybe it's not.

Perhaps if God removed His presence from some of our greatest biblical heroes, He also sometimes removes His presence from me and from you. And when that happens, it's okay to not immediately get back on that horse and ride or look for the lesson or celebrate the tough times that are "producing character." It's okay to mourn and scream and doubt and cry and question everything. And it's okay to tape yourself back together with the tape of your choice. (Within reason, of course. I am not in any way condoning illegal behavior, so please don't email me a stern admonishment.)

Life is hard. Tough times are going to come. Heartbreak is going to hit you. Loss is going to leave you reeling. People are going to abandon you. God might even turn His face from you. And when this happens, sometimes all you can do is hold on for dear life and SURVIVE. And maybe try and show yourself a little compassion and understanding through the process.

Because sometimes survival is about whatever gets you through the day. Whatever helps you put one foot in front of the other. Whatever holds you together when everything else falls apart.

Sometimes what holds you together is whiskey and Zoloft. Or a particular TV show or movie or book. Or a raggedy crew of misfits with whom you spend five and a half hours a day opening up your heart and letting it bleed in group therapy.

Sometimes what holds you together...is YOU.

And that's enough for the moment.

You Are Enough

I've kind of grown weary of the whole "everything happens for a reason" mentality, because often it seems like a very trite, cliché response to someone's pain. It almost seems to dismiss everything they've been through, by attempting to put a sparkly sheen on something that might have been very dark indeed. Sometimes it's okay to just let yourself feel the weight of what you're going through without trying to turn it into something *lighter. To let yourself accept the ugly without trying to turn it into something pretty. And to let yourself take a little time to cry instead of "smiling through the pain." Because the thing is, things do happen for reasons we sometimes can't possibly see or know or understand right at the moment they happen. Or ever. But through it all...we grow. We change. We evolve. We become the people we're meant to be. And perhaps that is the only reason that matters in the end, anyway. That doesn't mean we have to be happy about hard times or frantically try to put a positive spin on them to make ourselves feel better. It just means we can honor them for the way they changed us. The way they brought things out of us we didn't even know existed. The way they made us stronger, and better, and wiser. Yes, I think we can let hard times be exactly what they are without trying to find the "reason." Because the people we become through the surviving of the pain is far more important, and worthy of celebration and examination, than the pain itself.*

chapter 11

FINDING MYSELF

I started the partial hospitalization program (PHP) a few days after Christmas 2016. I walked in that first day more than a little nervous. This was completely different from IOP and at a new facility, so I had no frame of reference for what to expect. Plus I would be walking into a room of twenty or more strangers and expected to bare my soul and my innermost secrets for five and a half hours a day, five days a week. It felt a little bit like the first day of school. Nerves, anxiousness, dread, a little excitement, uncertainty. I was ready to begin the process of healing but also a little fearful of how difficult that process was going to be. I could no longer run from the problems that had been chasing me for almost three years now. I was going to be trapped in a room with no phone and no way to escape. It was time to face my feelings of rejection and worthlessness and self-doubt head-on.

After a lengthy one-on-one session with one of the counselors, I was turned loose to enter the group therapy room alone. The first session was already in progress, and the room was packed. It felt like all twenty-plus heads swiveled around to look at me when I walked in, self-conscious and trying to be as quiet as possible. *Will I be "enough" for this group of people, or will I fall short with them, too? Will I fit in? Will I be ostracized?* All of these thoughts were racing through my mind as I took my seat and listened to "check-ins."

I soon learned that every morning session kicked off with a check-in. We would go around the room and share how we were feeling, using descriptive terms, as well as how we slept the night before, what our goals were for the day, etc. Surprising even myself, I spoke up that first day and completed a check-in. After everyone had responded, we would take a short break and then split off into two different groups to begin the daily therapy sessions. Sometimes we would come back together as one big group during the course of the day, and sometimes not. We would take a lunch break at noon, and people who were in IOP would leave then. Those of us staying in PHP would have lunch together, then move on to afternoon sessions. It was structured very much like a school day, and there was a certain level of both relief and anxiety in that. Relief because the structure felt familiar and safe. Anxiety because *What if I don't have anyone to sit with or talk to? What if I am alienated by everyone and this process only serves to make me feel more alone?*

That first day when I looked around the circle of people, I was surprised and pleased to discover that everyone looked...well, normal. Like me. Some had very sad, grief-stricken eyes. Others were on the edges of their seats with anxiety. Most of us looked more than a little weary and exhausted. But we were all just normal people. Normal people who happened to be carrying the weight of depression or anxiety or some other mental illness. Normal people who had one very big thing in common: We wanted our lives back.

I was also happy to see a familiar face. As I scanned the room on day one, I saw the former neighbor of one of my best friends. Her name was Alex, and I had met her probably six or seven years earlier. We had even hung out a few times. Even though I was nervous and a little embarrassed (bumping into someone at the mental hospital isn't exactly the same as bumping into them at the grocery store), I approached Alex during a break and reintroduced myself. She seemed happy and a little relieved to see me, too. She had been in PHP for a few weeks and had just stepped down to IOP, so she would be leaving at noon every day. But still...I had someone to show me the ropes!

Isn't it funny how life always boils down to the basics? I was undergoing intensive therapy for soul-crushing depression, and my biggest concern those first few days was *Will I have someone to sit with? Will I fit in?* But I would soon come to see that those seemingly very simple questions were the foundation of a great many of my core problems. Never feeling like I fit. Never feeling like I belonged. Never feeling like I was lovable or wanted or needed. It was almost as though I went through my life looking for evidence that I wasn't any of those things. Waiting for someone to confirm that I was as much of a repellant as I often felt I was. Waiting for someone to prove once and for all that my worst fear in life—that I simply wasn't enough—was true.

And I began to realize, through group therapy, that for a long time, I had hidden behind my identity as "The Single Woman." I had derived my sense of self-worth from my career successes, my social media platforms, and the accolades and opportunities that came my way as a result. So when I no longer felt like I had a message to share or a publisher to help me share it, it was as though I lost a giant part of my identity in the process. No wonder the writing wasn't flowing anymore. I had no idea who I was or how to recapture the version of me that had written three books and inspired countless women across the world. It all felt overwhelming, the idea of letting people see the REAL me, exposing "the Mandy behind the curtain." I felt like that version of Mandy wasn't enough for my readers. (When, really, all you guys have ever asked me to be is me. I'm sorry I let my depression blind me to that fact.)

The really cool thing about group, though, was that no one knew who I was. I was just Mandy. I was a broken, insecure, unsure, often sad and anxious but REAL version of me, and it was okay. I was exactly who I was—no more, no less. I wasn't The Single Woman. I wasn't a *New York Times* best-selling author. I was just Mandy, a girl trying to find her way back from anxiety and depression. In group, I could say anything, feel anything, and no one judged me. I didn't have to say anything profound or wise or inspirational. I could cry. I could laugh. I could scream. I could refuse to participate altogether if I wanted to . . . and no one judged me.

It was an environment of complete and total unconditional acceptance unlike anything I had ever experienced in my life. And especially not in the past few years, since I had become a reluctant "public figure." Not to mention a Christian public figure. When you're a Christian public figure, there's just simply not a lot of room for meltdowns and identity crises. Maybe that's partially due to the pressure that I put on myself to "have it all together," but being in a safe space that allowed me to completely fall apart without fear of judgment was downright revolutionary for me.

Still, on day three of group, I woke up feeling overwhelmed and hopeless and scared. I didn't know if I could do it. I didn't know if I wanted to do it. I didn't know if I was ENOUGH to face up to all my demons and make it out on the other side unscathed. It was such an intense and vulnerable process. Spending almost six hours a day wading through the dark depths of emotions you've been running from for years is exhausting. I spent the day in bed, covers over my head, trying to block out the reality that I had been hiding from for so long.

The next day, I dragged myself out of bed and set out for group, determined to battle everything in me that wanted to give up and, instead, see this thing through.

That very day, a tiny woman in a purple scarf and with a gigantic personality walked into group for the first time and plopped down in the seat next to me. She had the saddest eyes I think I had ever seen but a distinctive laugh you could hear from a mile away. And she brought that laughter to everyone around her.

Her name was Shannon, and she had lost her beautiful seventeen-year-old daughter, Lucy, to suicide, a little over a year prior. She had been through unimaginable trauma and heartbreak and was somehow still standing, still fighting, still clawing her way back from the depths of despair.

She was, I knew within the first ten minutes of meeting her, the strongest person I had ever known.

Something that had eluded me for many years was a best friend. A TRUE best friend. A ride-or-die best friend. An "over a cliff" best friend. The Thelma to my Louise. The fact that this kind of friendship had never seemed to come easy for me was just one more thing that made me feel like I wasn't enough.

That fourth day of therapy, I had no idea that the tiny woman with the big personality would become the best friend I had ever had.

You Are Enough

There's something very powerful about that moment when we surrender our defenses, throw our hands up, and finally allow ourselves to cry, to feel, to admit that we have a broken heart. I don't know if it's the vulnerability of it all...the humility of it all...the fact that we're finally turning back to God because we've exhausted all of our other possibilities. But in those broken moments, we almost seem to rise up and become stronger, nobler, more ourselves than we've ever been before. Pretense goes out the window, and our authentic truth becomes our battle cry. And we become a vessel for God: We write with a passion like never before. We paint with a power like never before. We sing with a strength like never before. And through the cracks of our broken heart, God's spirit pours forth to heal our wounds. And ultimately, that same healing spirit also seals the cracks and leaves us stronger at the broken places. And better. And wiser. And brave enough to try again. Oh, the bittersweet beauty of a broken heart. Kinda makes you wonder why we run from the pain at all. I'm finding that we would do better to embrace it as just another stepping-stone to becoming who we're meant to be. Because the happy times might be great, but the sad times MAKE you great.

chapter 12

FAF

Friends are family. FAF. This concept would become as near and dear and familiar to me as my own initials over the next few months.

The days in group therapy went on. I continued to show up every single day and do the hard work, even when I didn't want to. We learned about codependence. We learned about radical acceptance. We learned about letting go and self-care and obsessive negative thoughts. We endured music therapy twice a week that we all hated and endlessly complained about.

With each passing day, I began to see just how deeply I had been wounded by Mr. E's rejection of me and of our relationship two years prior, and how that rejection had spilled over into every area of my life. A paralyzing fear of experiencing that same rejection again had frozen me in my tracks: emotionally, spiritually, physically, professionally. Always waiting for the other shoe to drop means you tiptoe your way through life, never taking chances, never risking anything, never experiencing real heartache but never experiencing real JOY either.

But because I'd experienced so much heartache and disappointment, the whirling, swirling storm of depression and anxiety was inevitable. I didn't understand why I seemed to have been dealt this hand that left me carrying the torch for singleness. It all began to feel like a sick joke. Like God had decided it was my lot in life to experience constant pain and disappointment and heartbreak so I could then turn around and help other people through it. My life's calling had been diminished to what felt like a cross to bear. And I felt like if people really saw who I was—behind the brand and the 140-character tweets and the sassy sayings—they, too, would see that I wasn't enough and would reject me for being me.

But now I was fully in a place where I was able to safely wrestle with all these big issues. And things, albeit slowly, started to change.

Not just because of the therapy. Not just because of medication. But because of the people surrounding me each day, listening to me, supporting me, propping me up when I felt I had nothing left to give, cheering me on for just simply being ME.

I began to connect with more people in group. Shannon was my biggest supporter and cheerleader, texting me encouraging messages at the end of the day, helping me overcome my fear of trying a new medication (I don't like taking medication at all), and constantly bringing me little gifts and surprises at group to bring a smile to my face. As the days passed by, as December turned into January and January became February, something began to happen among that group of people at Whispering Pines. Some sort of something I can only describe as...magic. We were all at our lowest, most broken points, some of us feeling like we had lost absolutely everything, and yet we found each other. We truly found love in a hopeless place. Out of the barren soil of our despair began to grow the most beautiful little flowers of friendship. We celebrated each other's victories. We cried with each other in moments of defeat. We honored the space we were in, no matter how sad or discouraged we might be that day. We threw celebratory lunches when someone graduated from the program. Yes, somewhere along the way, in the midst of our hardest days, we became a family.

"Friends are family" became our mantra, "FAF" for short. "You got this!" was one of our favorite phrases to encourage one another. Whether it was opening up to someone in our lives about what we were going through, or applying for a new job, or simply making it through another day, we pumped each other up with "You got this!" Usually followed by a fist bump (or a fist-bump emoji, if we were texting). I began to look around myself and marvel at the beauty of the vulnerability and honesty that ran through our group. *THIS is how church and home groups and Bible study groups should feel,* I thought. REAL. Raw. Unfiltered. No masks. No walls. And no apologies for your brokenness. Because the truth is, most people sitting in church pews every Sunday are just as broken as my friends from group and I were. They are just terrified to admit it.

My faith, which had taken quite a hit over the past few months, began to slowly reawaken from the hibernation it had been in. Though I had long ago stopped seeing a reflection of Jesus in most churches I visited—with their strobe lights, and hipster pastors in skinny jeans, and fancy coffee bars—I started to see Him again in the faces of my group family. That might sound strange, given that most of us were a little rough around the edges, had an affinity for four-letter words, and were more about holey jeans than holy genes (at least in this season of our lives), but it was true. We listened to one another. We loved one another well. We supported one another. One mom in the group even offered to do the young twentysomethings' laundry for them. It was messy, beautiful, unconditional love at its finest. And it reintroduced me to Jesus. The fierce and unconditional and rough-around-the-edges Jesus. How I had missed Him so.

I had never been more broken, and I had never been more ENOUGH.

My healing came slowly and not as swiftly as my heartbreak had, but it came. It came thanks to the wonderful staff at Whispering Pines, many hours of therapy, a little help from medication...but mostly thanks to my group family. My FAF crew. My motley band of fellow raggedy misfits that gave me, for perhaps the first time in my life, a place to BELONG.

One night in late January 2017, we all planned a night out on the town. We went dancing at a place called Crazy Town in Nashville (the irony of the name wasn't lost on us). Shannon even brought out her famous twerking. (She became known in our group as Twerkin' Shannon.) To see this group of friends, all races and sexes and walks of life, ages eighteen all the way to fiftysomething, laughing and dancing and having the time of their lives, you would never know for a second that anything was wrong. That they had spent the past two months undergoing intensive therapy for various mental health issues. You probably would never imagine for a second that most of them had known each other for only two months. You'd think they were old friends, or maybe even family.

And in a way, you'd be right.

The night was ours, and we lived every moment to the last drop. I got home in the wee hours of the morning, happier than I had been in months.

A couple of weeks later, it was Valentine's Day, and the day before I was set to graduate from Whispering Pines. My "little sister" from group, Grace, approached me shyly after morning check-ins with something concealed behind her back. Grace was battling her way back from severe depression and more than one suicide attempt, yet she always managed to have the biggest smile on her face, bright enough to light up a room. She had been hurt a lot, so she was emotionally guarded and not incredibly open about telling people how she felt about them. But that day, she handed me the stuffed teddy bear she had picked out for me so I wouldn't have to endure yet another Valentine's Day without receiving a gift, and I knew how much our friendship meant to her. I can only hope she knew how much her gesture and that little teddy bear meant to me.

It was all so wonderfully, beautifully ENOUGH.

And after almost two months of intensive therapy, wrestling with some great big scary emotions, meeting my problems head-on, and finding a family that had given so much back to me: my hope, my faith, my healing, my sense of wholeness...

I finally felt like *I* was enough, too.

Group therapy was the hardest, most challenging, most rewarding process of my life. And it was over. But the rest of my life was just beginning.

You Are Enough

Because one day in the middle of your brokenness, you'll look around and realize that you're smiling. And this being-leveled-right-down-to-the-foundation stuff won't look sad *and empty...It will look hopeful. And suddenly, losing everything you thought you wanted will look less like loss and more like room. Room for new things and people and places and opportunities. Room to stretch and grow and bloom. Room to be YOU.*

Did you know that sunflowers are called sunflowers because they literally turn toward the sun? One day you'll wake up and the storm will have finally quieted, and you'll find yourself turning and stretching and reaching toward the sun. And the darkness won't seem so overwhelming anymore, now that you've identified the light. And being lost won't look so overwhelming anymore; it will simply look like finding yourself, finding a new way—one of your own, one that no one else charted before you. On that day when you look around and you no longer recognize your life, it won't scare you anymore. It will inspire you. And all of a sudden, your cracks and scars won't look like flaws at all. They'll look like beauty marks.

chapter 13

THE TIME OF MY LIFE

I've always been a sucker for a romantic comedy. Or a romantic dramedy. Or, really, a romantic movie of any kind. From a very young age, I was mesmerized by motion pictures, but particularly ones that dealt with matters of the heart. In fifth grade, my teacher would turn on *Gone with the Wind* every day during snack time, and though we only got to watch it for about fifteen minutes a day (which meant it took forever to get all the way through it), it was the highlight of my day. Of course, *Gone with the Wind* is pretty far removed from a romantic comedy! But still...watching lovelorn Scarlett O'Hara moon over Ashley Wilkes while the dapper and dashing Rhett Butler stood waiting in the wings just set my soul on fire.

When I was a little older, an independent film you may have heard of called *Dirty Dancing* was released, and although my parents wouldn't let my sister and me go see it at the theater, it would become the first movie we would ever rent on videotape (yes, kids...this was before the age of DVDs and Blu-rays and Netflix and Amazon). My dad even bought us a VCR for the occasion, which in those days was a really big deal. And even though my mom and dad made us fast-forward through the sexy parts, the film captivated me like nothing ever had before. I was in love with movies. I was in love with LOVE. I was in love with the wonder of it all, the coming-of-age of it all, the idea that a routine vacation with your family to the mountains could alter the course of your entire life and drop you right smack-dab into the middle of a fairy-tale romance. Because of the movie and its impact on me, I began to believe in magic and whimsy and serendipity and fate like never before. I began to dream and wish and hope and imagine. In all seriousness, I truly believe *Dirty Dancing* changed the course of my life and even helped set me on the path to someday becoming a writer and spinning my own tales of love and happily ever after.

As I got older, I began to realize that one of the things about romantic movies that struck a chord with me the most was "the grand gesture." You know, that moment at the end of the film where the guy chases the girl (or the girl chases the guy) to the airport, the train station, etc. to declare their love. Or in *Dirty Dancing*–speak, the "Nobody puts Baby in a corner" moment. I began to wish for and hope for and dream about having my own Johnny Castle to sweep me off my feet in true grand-gesture fashion.

And somewhere in the midst of my wishing and hoping and dreaming, I met a boy who loved to dance. A boy who lit up my world. A boy whom you all know as Mr. E. A boy who even traveled with me to one of the locations where *Dirty Dancing* was filmed in North Carolina. If you've read my second book, *I've Never Been to Vegas but My Luggage Has*, you'll remember this moment. We found the steps where Baby practiced her dance moves, and that boy kissed me right there in that very spot, setting my little movie-nerd heart aflutter.

But every high moment with that boy was followed by an even lower moment—leading me to finally come to a conclusion one night, as we sat in Grand Central Terminal in New York City, where so many cinematic grand-gesture moments have been filmed, and I asked him: "You're never gonna be that guy at the end of the movie who chases me, are you?"

The answer was no.

And he would prove that, time and time and time again, over the course of nearly a decade.

So when the curtain finally closed on our relationship for seemingly the last time, and his cruel words sent me spiraling, I put away my romantic movies: My old friends. My sources of inspiration. My reminders that great big love and great big gestures can and do exist...if only in our imagination.

I began to doubt love. For the first time in my life, I questioned whether or not there was really a happy ending out there for me. I looked around at other people and wondered why love seemed to come so easily for them and yet be so unattainable for me. I put walls up around my heart. I closed myself off emotionally. I shut down. For a dreamer and an idealist like me, someone who lived with my head in the clouds, to stop dreaming and imagining and looking for magic and believing in Hollywood endings was detrimental to my spirit. My creativity took a hit. My personal relationships suffered. My world became very small. I was no longer the person I had always been. I wasn't sure who I was, honestly. It's no wonder I spiraled into deep depression.

To be disappointed in love, over and over and over again, can cause us to stop believing and dreaming and hoping and wishing. It can cause us to grow cynical. It can harden us. It can make us retreat inward and shut other people out until we look up one day and find ourselves all alone. For me, movies had always been my saving grace. Why movies, you might ask? They're not based in reality. They're make-believe. And yet . . . life imitates art, and art imitates life. It's this beautiful, perfect circle. And I've found that often, when you have an open heart and eyes to see, life and God find ways to bring you breathtaking, awe-inspiring moments that surpass anything you've ever seen on a movie screen.

For two years, my eyes were closed. My hands were closed. My heart was closed. And then, like they always have, movies once again found a way to creep back in and become my guiding light. In my research over the years into the filming of *Dirty Dancing*, I had discovered that the resort that served as Kellerman's in the movie is an actual place you can go and stay. It's called Mountain Lake Lodge, and it's located in the beautiful mountains of Pembroke, Virginia. It had always been on my bucket list to go visit, and in early spring 2017, after the difficult year my family and I had had, I decided there was no time like the present. I mean, what a great way to celebrate my graduation from Whispering Pines, right?

Arriving at Mountain Lake Lodge was just like stepping into the movie. It's exactly like Kellerman's. From Baby's cabin (which you can actually rent!) to the lake to the gazebo to the main dining hall, you can feel the spirit of the movie all around you. And even beyond just getting to nerd out over being on hallowed *Dirty Dancing* ground, the resort itself is breathtakingly beautiful and peaceful and serene. It was precisely what my soul needed at that moment in time.

Because Baby and Johnny's lake (where they practiced the lift) has receded over the years, you actually have to hike out a pretty good distance to see it. I decided to take this hike by myself one day, in order to have an opportunity to spend some time alone and soak in the atmosphere.

When I got out to the lake, I found a bench right by the water. It made for a perfect spot to sit and reflect on the gravity of the fact that due to the water's recession since the movie was filmed, I was basically sitting in the middle of the lake where the fictional couple I loved so much had started to fall in love.

Something about that caused my closed-off heart to begin to open, just a tiny bit.

And as I sat and pondered the past two years and how guarded I had become...and the past few months and the depths of hopelessness and despair I had experienced...and the previous thirty-six years before that and how unguarded and open and hopeful I had been...and as I whispered words to God and felt the cool lake breeze tickle my face and marveled at the ecstatic dance of joy my eleven-year-old self must be doing somewhere in time to see her all-grown-up self sitting by the lake where she had been in her imagination so many times before...something in me changed. The carefully formed walls I had erected around myself—not just since The Boy Upstairs had left but since Mr. E had devastated me two years before—began to crack. I began to feel the first rays of hope shine down upon me like the warm spring sun. And it suddenly occurred to me that if I could spend all those years loving the wrong person, get my heart broken beyond measure, endure crushing depression and undergo intensive therapy, and yet still be standing, still have enough childlike faith to find magic in a place that to anyone else might just be your average lake (and a dried-up one at that!), and still tap into that part of me that believed in love and movie moments and grand gestures and fairy tales...wasn't anything possible? Wasn't it conceivable that maybe there was still a Hollywood ending out there for me, too?

I took a rock from Baby and Johnny's lake that day, a touchstone I keep with me now to remind me of that moment, of all the things I really, truly believe in, of the girl I was before life and hurt and heartbreak and disappointment and depression came in and changed her. And of the girl I am now: a little bit stronger, a little bit wiser, but still a dreamer who, despite the setbacks and the struggles, still sees life as a beautiful, wondrous adventure.

It had been a year since I'd encountered that wise stranger who told me: "When you lose yourself, you find yourself." It had been almost a year since my brother-in-law's accident. And what a year it had been. I think I needed to lose myself for a little while, to wander, to wonder, in order to realize that I will always, always be able to find myself again in the things that I love. In the things that I've always loved. The heart of who we are, who we WERE, way back when—it never really changes. It just gets covered up sometimes by the storms and uncertainties and hardships of life.

I knew that whether or not love ever found me, I was well on my way to finding myself again. That little girl who watched nobody put Baby in a corner with wide eyes and believed that she, too, was enough? Was inherently lovable? Was worthy of a grand gesture? Turns out she was still in there. How I had missed her. And as crazy as it might sound, I'm not sure I would have found her or, for that matter, ever become her in the first place, without a little movie called *Dirty Dancing*.

As it turns out, a routine vacation to the mountains with your family can, in fact, alter the course of your entire life.

Maybe in this case, I made my own grand gesture by visiting the place where the movie that had captivated me for most of my life was filmed. Maybe I rescued myself. Maybe, in the end, we have to learn to rescue ourselves. Maybe that's what real love is all about. Hoping and dreaming and wishing to someday dance wildly with a partner...

But learning and loving to dance, just as wildly, without one.

You Are Enough

And one night as you're strolling down a sidewalk somewhere, perhaps eating an ice-cream cone that drips just a bit in the warm spring breeze, thinking rather wistfully to yourself, My, how romantic this would be, walking hand in hand down this Technicolor sidewalk with someone I love, *it will suddenly come to you: Why do we always wait for someone else to bring us romance? And why do we always feel as though our lives are lacking it just because we might not have a romantic partner? Perhaps this moment, this very moment right now, is romantic, simply because there is a hint of magic in the air and breath in your lungs and a smile on your face. Maybe you and I don't need anyone at all to bring us romance. We only need open eyes to see it and an open heart to feel it and open arms to receive it. Maybe, just maybe, romance and happiness and love are all around us, regardless of whether we're walking with someone, or completely alone. And maybe, just maybe, our enoughness, our worth, has nothing whatsoever to do with who's beside us and everything to do with what's inside us.*

chapter 14

AN UNEXPECTED APOLOGY

*M*y time in group therapy, my work in individual therapy, and my own self-reflection while visiting Mountain Lake helped me reach an important decision in early spring 2017. It was time to reach out to Mr. E. It was time to go back to the start of it all, the event that sent me spiraling, more than two years earlier, and attempt to find some clarity and closure. It was time to stop hiding from the biggest ghost from my past and instead face him head-on. The lingering feelings of regret and rejection and betrayal would never fully be put to rest until I had a chance to say the things I had been holding in for years and to ask for an explanation for the horrible things he had said to me. The things that had scarred me so badly they left me questioning everything about myself and set my life on a different path. Maybe I wouldn't get an explanation that satisfied me, or one at all, but at least I could try.

I should pause right here and say that from this moment forward, Mr. E will be referred to as John. It's not his real name, of course, but I feel like it's time to stop shrouding him in fanciful layers of mystery that only serve to romanticize his eternal evasiveness. "Evasive" and "indirect" and "unclear about his intentions" are not qualities I want to celebrate any longer in a potential romantic partner. So...John it is.

I went the safe route in reaching out to him: a Facebook message. I wasn't ready to risk sending a text. At least if someone doesn't reply to a Facebook message, you can convince yourself they never saw it. I kept it very simple, just saying hi and that I had been thinking about him. And then I waited. Nervously. I wanted closure, even needed closure, but I was also still very much in the process of healing, and I wasn't sure how another rejection, even one in the form of an unreturned Facebook message, would impact me.

A day went by, then another. No response.

On day three, I retreated to my happy place, or one of them, anyway: Target. Whenever anything is going wrong or I'm struggling to make a decision or wrestling with matters of the heart, I head to either Target or Barnes & Noble. Usually a few hours at either place will set me straight again (and also set me back a hundred bucks or so, since I usually leave Target with new dish towels, a lamp, a onesie, a new curling iron, and a partridge in a pear tree). I was roaming the aisles aimlessly when my phone buzzed. It was him. John. Replying to my Facebook message.

At first, he just sort of rambled on, making small talk. I replied back, also keeping things generic and light. Then, out of the blue, the next set of messages came through, like someone had opened a floodgate: *If reaching out to me wasn't a sign of forgiveness, then please forgive me. I regret that day. I was all wrong. I am very sorry I hurt your heart.*

I stopped cold in the middle of the store, completely breathless, speechless, motionless. The albatross of more than two years of angst and pain and self-doubt and torment and questioning myself over and over and over again that had sat on my shoulders... in an instant... felt lighter. His apology didn't completely erase everything I had been through, obviously, but it definitely eased the burden of blame I had heaped on myself when he told me he didn't love me anymore. *Why wasn't I enough for him?* I had been asking for these past two years. Turns out it wasn't about me at all. It was never about me. Wow. (Spoiler alert: A man's bad behavior is almost NEVER about us, ladies.)

I didn't seek you out for an apology, I replied. *But I also had no idea how much I needed one.*

I needed to get rid of that apology a long time ago, he wrote back. *It has been heavy for far too long. I needed to let it go, too. I couldn't apologize before you gave me permission to talk to you. Maybe I could have. But I couldn't.*

You did hurt my heart, I told him. *It took a very long time to heal. And I didn't think I would ever want or be ready to talk to you again. But time heals all, as they say. It really does. And you're a big part of my history. You're a big part of my writing. You're a big part of me. And you always will be. So yes, I accept and appreciate your apology. And I forgive you.*

Thank you, he replied. *I have to breathe now. That has taken a large portion of my attention since you first said hi. I am feeling next to wordless.*

By that point, I was sitting in the next-to-empty Target café, tears streaming down my face. I had received an apology I didn't ask for and didn't even know I needed. It was such a cathartic moment.

Those kinds of moments tend to be pretty rare in this life, apologies from former loves who broke your heart. Turns out for every moment I had suffered from heartbreak, John had suffered from regret. And now both of us could breathe a little easier again. You don't really realize the weight of the load you're carrying until you set it down, I suppose. And sitting there, in the Target café, I finally set down a burden I had been carrying for more than two years. The root of it all—the depression, the anxiety, the heart palpitations, the raging self-doubt and questioning of my worth and blaming myself for never being enough for love—was that moment on my couch when the man I had loved with my whole heart for almost eight years brutally and completely rejected me. And now I realized that John had spent more than two years wishing he could take back every hurtful thing he had said just as much as I wished he had never said it.

Neither of us could erase or take back the past or the things we had been through, but we could move forward in the present. And we did. The next night, we talked on the phone for several hours, and he was able to further explain his actions on that fateful day. He said he had acted from a place of hurt, based on what he perceived as my rejection of him during our ill-fated attempt at a long-distance relationship in 2014. And though that doesn't excuse his actions, it certainly helped me understand a little better where he was coming from. And that his own fears and self-doubts and attempts to avoid getting hurt had seemingly caused him to lash out and reject me before I could reject him. Relationships are so complicated, with everyone hiding behind their various defense mechanisms and allowing ghosts from the past to haunt their relationships in the present. It's a miracle any of us ever end up on the same page at the same time.

But for the moment, it seemed, John and I were on the same page at the same time. We began talking on the phone every day. We had the beginnings of what felt like a solid friendship. He was still living in Boone, North Carolina, running his family's business, so it was once again a long-distance friendship (which seemed to be the only way we knew how to do things), but he mentioned more than once the idea of coming to Tennessee to see me. Of course, I felt those same old feelings start to come back…but I was trying to proceed with caution and not jump into anything too fast, especially since I didn't know exactly how he was feeling.

And then, quite suddenly, he made his feelings crystal clear.

I answered the phone one night to hear him crying. I had witnessed this level of emotion from him only once or twice in the decade that I had known him, so I was surprised and concerned, to say the least. "What's going on?" I asked him, worried.

He told me he had realized over these past couple of weeks since we started talking again that he was madly in love with me and that I was the person he wanted to spend his life with. That he had been too afraid to tell me he loved me for years, but that he couldn't hold it in any longer. That I was the person he wanted to marry, and that he had no doubts about that anymore. It had taken him ten years, but he finally knew what he wanted. And what he wanted, he said, was me.

I'd love to say I was levelheaded and discerning and guarded and I responded in a measured, cautious way...but who are we kidding? I'm a hopeless romantic, and I always will be. Time and heartache and even depression hadn't managed to steal that away from me. And here was the man I had loved for the better part of a decade telling me he wanted to spend his life with me. My every movie-moment fantasy wrapped into one great big romantic package. It suddenly felt like everything that came before made perfect sense, like this is where we were always destined to end up, like every moment John and I had been through so far was leading us to this one.

As usual, I let my heart get ahead of my head. I forgot, in an instant, everything I knew to be true about John—that he was great at grand gestures and movie moments but not so great at everyday, ordinary life.

I jumped in with both feet.

You Are Enough

You didn't know. You trusted, and you loved, and you assumed the best of someone . . . and that is never wrong. You took a shot at love or at friendship . . . and that is always brave. You believed that the other person would treat you with the same dignity and respect with which you treated them . . . and that is noble.

You didn't know. You didn't know they weren't capable of loving you back. You didn't know they weren't trustworthy. You didn't know they didn't have the capacity or the character to handle your heart with the same care with which you handled theirs.

You didn't know. You didn't have all the information that you have now. If you had, you might have chosen differently . . . and the truth is, sometimes in life and in love it takes standing too close to the fire to learn how not to get burned.

So forgive yourself for not making different choices. Because good choices make you happy, but bad choices make you better and stronger. Keep being the brave, trusting person that you are, because someday the right person will love you for it instead of exploiting you for it.

You didn't know. Forgive yourself for not knowing.

Forgive them for what they did.

And let it go, armed with the beautiful knowledge that comes from going out on a limb, regardless of whether you fall or fly.

chapter 15

WHEN LOVE DIES

As one love of my life was beginning to bloom, another love of my life was fading away. In April 2017, John and I were on a path that seemed to be leading straight to, well...happily ever after. At the same time, my precious grandmother, Nanny, was in the hospital, fighting for her life. Nanny had suffered a stroke about eight years earlier that left her bedridden but still with all her mental faculties. Over the last few months, however, her health had slowly started to deteriorate. The slightest cold or bug could send her to the hospital for weeks on end. This time, she seemed particularly fragile, and the thought of losing her was weighing heavily on all our minds.

Nanny was the perfect grandmother. The quintessential Southern lady. She was the best cook I'd ever met, she had a heart of gold and a soul of sunshine, and she was a devout Christian woman who called all of her six children and fifteen grandchildren out by name in prayer every night. She had known great hardship and loss in her life and yet, still, she persevered. She and my grand-daddy were married for seventy years before he passed away. She was strong and beautiful and loving and good.

And she was a writer. Not a published one, mind you...but a few years ago my mom and my aunts came across some old writings of hers in a drawer and shared them with me. I was blown away by her passion and vulnerability and eloquence. She wrote poems mostly. And I was surprised and pleased to discover that the tone of her writings had a similar feel to my work. It brought me great joy and pride to know that even though she might have never had the opportunity to have her words published, her granddaughter had and was carrying the torch for her in a way. She used to tell me all the time: "Mandy Bear, God has something very special planned for you." From the time I was born until I was a grown woman, she never wavered in her belief that God had great plans for me.

She was right, of course. Her granddaughter would one day speak into the lives of women all across the world. She had her stroke before my writing career really took off, but she still beamed with pride the day I took a signed copy of my first book to her bedside. She might not have been able to physically be at my book signings, but her spirit was always with me, everywhere I went—every stage, every platform, every TV appearance. The fervent prayers of Emily Jean Reed Frost always helped carry me through even my biggest and most anxiety-inducing moments (live television and public speaking both terrify me).

And then we were told in mid-April 2017 that Nanny wouldn't ever make it home from the hospital. Her doctor said she was simply too weak this time and she wouldn't be able to recover from the pneumonia that had sent her there. We were told it was time to say our good-byes.

Since John and I were essentially back together and discussing marriage, I told him I wanted him to try to come to Tennessee to meet Nanny before she passed. It might seem fast, but we had known each other for ten years now. There wasn't the awkward getting-to-know-you phase to get through. And with Nanny being my last remaining grandparent, it was hugely important to me for her to meet the man who I had begun to believe was "my person" before she passed. Even if she didn't fully realize who he was, it would still mean something to me. John promised he would be there. We decided on that upcoming weekend for his visit, which would also be Easter weekend. We thought it would be nice to not only introduce John to Nanny but also to have that time together and attend church together on Sunday.

The weekend rolled around. I was obviously heart-broken about Nanny but still over the moon to get to see

John. He was supposed to be there on Friday. He first called me that afternoon to tell me he was going to have to delay until that night so he could finish something at work. A loud warning bell went off in my gut, but I tried to drown it out and give him the benefit of the doubt. Later that night, as I was grocery shopping for his impending arrival, he called to tell me he would have to head my way on Saturday morning instead.

You can probably guess what happened next.

Saturday turned into Sunday...and still no John.

He flaked on me. For one of the most important moments of my life—meeting my precious grandmother before she died. He didn't show up. He had nothing to give me but excuses.

Nothing had really changed with John. Nothing would ever change. I knew that now. Regardless of his grand words and grand gestures, his actions were as scared and small and spineless as always.

I had bought a new green dress for John's visit, because he liked me in green. On Easter Sunday I got up, put on the green dress anyway, and went to spend the day with my Nanny. The rest of my family was there, too. It would be the last day we would ever spend with her.

On that day, my brother-in-law, a giant of a man, kneeled down next to my grandmother and spoke softly to her. He talked to her about going fishing, because he knows she loved to fish, and he patted her head and held her hand and told her he loved her. Because that's what love does. It shows up, and it meets you right where you're at. Love kneels and comforts and speaks softly of hope even when all hope seems lost.

And my dad sacrificed time and sleep for a solid week to stand not only by my grandmother's bedside but also by my mom's side. Because that's what love does. It sacrifices. It misses out on sleep. It puts the other person ahead of its own comfort. LOVE SHOWS UP.

On that final Easter morning with my Nanny, on a day in which we were celebrating sacrificial love, my heart was heavy, because I knew, once and for all, that I hadn't found that kind of love in John. My grandmother was leaving us, and I knew she would never get to meet my future husband or my children. She would never be at my wedding. She would never get to see how my life, which she had prayed over for all these years, turned out. She wouldn't be there to celebrate with me when I found my happy ending.

And my happy ending wasn't going to be with John.

But then I looked over at my dad and my brother-in-law, and I felt a tiny spark of hope that maybe someday a man like them might join our tribe and stand by my side. A real man. A man who doesn't run when times get hard. A man who stands and faces whatever storms life brings our way with a face set like flint. A man who is steady and solid and there for me to lean on when I'm sad, or broken, or lost. A man who puts love first. A man who always makes me feel like I am completely and totally ENOUGH.

A man like Jesus.

And, no, he won't ever get to meet my precious grandmother. But he'll hear stories about her and how she prayed for me. And how those fervent prayers of a faithful grandmother helped bring him to me. Helped him find me and me find him.

Someday this man would complete the picture. He would complete our family. It wouldn't be that day. But someday.

I whispered something in my Nanny's ear before I left her that day, words I've never revealed to anyone until now. Though she was near-comatose, I told her I had a favor to ask her. To my surprise, she nodded her head yes. "Nanny," I said, "can you please ask Jesus when you see Him to bring me the right man? Because I'm sure not having any luck finding him on my own, and my heart is weary from looking." She nodded yes again. I kissed her and said goodbye.

Those would be the last words I ever spoke to her. Later that night, Nanny went to be with Jesus.

She might not have brought me my mate yet, but I don't doubt for a second that she played a role in keeping me from ending up with the wrong person.

John would have been wrong for me. It took him flaking on me and breaking my heart once again during one of the most heartbreaking moments of my life for me to see that.

A couple of months prior, had the same thing happened, I would have most definitely folded. I would have crashed. I would have ended up in bed for days on end, questioning what I had done wrong and why I wasn't enough for John. And why I had to lose him and my beloved Nanny all at the same time.

But that was then. This was now. I had been through a fire or two, and I knew I was enough for whatever life threw at me.

That truth and my grandmother's strength in my spine is what kept me going.

You Are Enough

Lost boys, broken boys, dishonest boys, unavailable boys... I've spent way too much time in my life chasing after the wrong guys. Guys who didn't know or love themselves enough to ever possibly know or love me. Guys who were so hopelessly, desperately lost they used parts of my soul as bread crumbs to try and find their way back. Guys who were drowning in their own lives and grasping for a life raft. But you know what happens to girls who allow themselves to become life rafts? They sink themselves. They get dragged into whirling, swirling cesspools of drama and chaos and dysfunction. They start to mistake mirages for the real deal. They start to question why they seem to never be ENOUGH.

So the next time a lost boy tries to take your hand and lead you down his path of confusion, politely say no. Or even impolitely say no. But say no. You are not a life raft, you are not a compass, you are not bread crumbs, you are not a flashlight, you are not a Band-Aid, and you are not a stop along the way as he attempts to "find himself." You are a destination. A whole, complete person who deserves another whole, complete person. You are wonderfully, beautifully ENOUGH. Too enough for someone who can't see what he has standing right in front of his face.

Maybe you're saying, "Hey, I'm a little lost right now, too." And that's okay. But find your own way. Chart your own course. And never use another human being and their feelings and emotions as your GPS. Never look to another person to rescue you. Rescue yourself. Then you won't even attract the lost boys anymore. You'll attract the found ones.

chapter 16

WHY WE CLING TO PEOPLE WHO DON'T LOVE US

Why did I cling to a man who didn't love me for ten years?

I had to ask myself some hard questions in the days following my grandmother's passing and the final chapter of John and me. If I was to continue my path of healing and wholeness, I could no longer run from harsh realities. I felt like I could finally see things so clearly, as if I were someone now standing on the inside, looking out. I guess you have to be really ready to see someone for who they really are. Until that moment, until the veil finally lifts, you find yourself making excuse after excuse after excuse for them. Is that you right now? Is that where you're at?

Let me tell you some of the thoughts that went

through my mind during my decade of waiting for John to love me:

He doesn't know how to handle his feelings. They're too intense. He runs whenever he has serious feelings for someone. He's emotionally immature. He's scared of commitment. He loves me SO much he doesn't know how to express it.

He's so different from other guys. I can't apply hard-and-fast He's Just Not That into You *rules to John, because he's one of a kind. When God made him, He broke the mold. If I just wait a little longer, he'll wake up and realize how he feels about me and we'll live happily ever after.*

He moved across the country / disappeared / stopped calling me because we started to get too close. Anytime we get too close, he runs. His feelings for me are overwhelming, so that's why he vanishes.

I know he's the one for me. I know I just have to be patient, just give him a little more time. He moves slowly when he's really serious about someone. He committed only to wildly inappropriate girls in the past because he knew it wouldn't last. Yes, that's why he committed to them and not me... because he knows I'm a keeper, and once he commits to me, it's forever. That has to be it. I'm the one for him and he knows it, and we have such an intense connection it's scary to him. He runs because he's scared. He doesn't commit to me because he's scared. He flakes because he's scared. He drifts in and out of my life because he's scared.

Maybe I'm just not enough for him. Maybe I'm too much. Maybe if I change this, this, or this about myself... I'll finally BE enough and he'll finally see how much he loves me.

Of course, reading all that now, today, it's easy for me to see the sheer insanity of my thought process. But this is what we do. We can't admit the truth to ourselves because it's too painful. So instead we write the story for the other person. We fill in the gaps with soft, shiny, protective denial because the sharp edges of the truth hurt too much. We look for deeper, hidden, more noble meanings to their every word because we can't face up to the truth that their actions are showing us exactly how they feel. We let them off the hook time and time and time again for letting us down and breaking our hearts because we just know that underneath it all, underneath the pretense and over the giant wall they've erected all around them, beats the heart of a person deeply in love with us. We don't take their actions at face value because the face looking back at us is too cold and distant and removed for us to recognize…and the person we've invested so much time and emotion and energy into would NEVER be cold and distant and removed. Would they?

The truth is, my friends, there's no such thing as loving someone too much to be with them. No such thing as being so overwhelmed by your feelings for someone that you run from them. As being too scared to commit to someone. These are the stories that perhaps some men want us to believe, because they're fraught with drama and romanticism and tortured passion…but the truth is far, far simpler.

When someone shows you how they feel…or don't feel about you…believe them.

If they love you, they'll act like it. If they're not acting like it…they don't love you.

If they want to be with you ... they'll be with you. They won't just SAY they want to be with you or tell their friends they want to be with you ... They'll SHOW you. They won't profess their love to you and tell you they want to marry you and then cruelly turn around and flake on you when you ask them to come meet your dying grandmother.

If their words say one thing and their actions say another ... believe their actions. Every time.

The truth, even when it comes to love, is far simpler than we dare imagine or even wish. If you are left with feelings of confusion and anguish and uncertainty and rejection and unease, that isn't love. Love isn't perfect, no, but it's also not torturous. It's not painful. It's not a constant gray area. Love is certain. Love looks like love. Love doesn't hide or dodge or run. Love shows up. Love makes itself known, and it makes itself clear.

It took me a decade to understand that anyone you have to wait around for to love you is someone who will never love you. There isn't going to come this magical day when they suddenly wake up and realize they love you. There isn't going to be this grand gesture where they chase you to the airport or the train station to confess their true feelings for you. You can waste years of your life waiting for the grand gesture. I did. And if they have the desire to run when you come around, it isn't because their feelings for you are so intense they don't know how to handle them. It's because they don't know how to handle telling you that their feelings aren't all that intense.

This truth will make some people uncomfortable. It will make some people mad. Others will read it, dismiss it, and stay with feet and heart firmly planted in that endless purgatory of waiting for someone to love them.

But maybe, just maybe, it will also wake a few people up. Maybe it will empower one or two people to slam a door shut once and for all and not look back. Maybe it will save someone from wasting ten years of their life on the wrong person, like I did. Maybe it will keep someone out there from questioning everything about themselves and doubting their very worth as a human being just because one guy didn't know how to get his act together.

I'm not sure why I waited so long for someone to love me back who was never capable of it. Maybe because I didn't love myself enough to see that I deserved so much more. Maybe because I didn't want to admit to myself that someone I cared about so deeply didn't share my feelings. Maybe I was simply scared to let him go because I was afraid of what that feeling of holding on to nothing felt like. (Even though I was already essentially holding on to nothing; I just didn't realize it for a really long time.) Or maybe it was because for many years, I didn't feel worthy and deserving of great love. I didn't feel like I was ENOUGH.

Or maybe it was because I was always meant to write this book and remind you that maybe, just maybe, it's not YOU who isn't enough for HIM. Perhaps it's HIM who's not enough for YOU.

You Are Enough

You can learn to coexist with those moments of sadness without letting them take you under. You can accept that some people will perhaps forever remain in your heart but not in your life. You can choose to stop trying to force your brain not to actively think about him, which makes you only think about him more, and instead let the thoughts in with the caveat that you're going to let them linger only long enough to send him love and light, and maybe whisper a brief prayer on his behalf, and then you're going to drop it. That's how you move on. That's how you let go. Realizing that you are ENOUGH, with or without that person in your life. Divine acceptance of all that is, and all that will never be, and a dash of surrender on the side. Arms, hands, and heart wide-open is a very powerful stance. When you surrender something, you're not denying that it once meant a great deal to you. You're just giving back to God what is no longer yours.

chapter 17

MOVING ON

*I*t was almost summer, and I was still in apartment 33, i.e., the apartment two doors down from The Boy Upstairs. Though everything in my life had changed, and I was growing and evolving and healing, and facing down hard times without letting them defeat me, and learning to embrace my enoughness, I was still physically stuck in the same location. And it was affecting my emotional well-being. When you make big changes on the inside, your outer surroundings need to match up. Mine didn't. I felt restless and frustrated and trapped in the past. I knew I wouldn't be able to fully continue my journey of healing and wholeness until I found a space to live in that felt more like ME. The me that I was finally learning to accept was ENOUGH, just as I was.

I began to seek God's direction on a new place to live. I wanted somewhere in the same area, as I loved living close to the town square, but I wanted more space and light. I wanted a place that felt warm and cozy and safe. A place that would be a peaceful retreat from the world around me when life got too crazy. A place that felt like HOME. Within a few days of having a chat with God about what I was looking for in a new place, I felt compelled to take one of my morning walks down to the square. And that's how I stumbled upon my new apartment. An apartment that if I closed my eyes and pictured my perfect living environment, would be it. It was in an old historic home, it was big and airy and bright, it had a killer balcony that overlooked Main Street, and it was beautifully decorated and even came furnished if I wanted it to. Best of all, it was in my price range.

A few days later, the apartment was mine.

I have learned in my life that the things meant for me usually come looking for me. I have never had to strive or force or manipulate to receive what is truly for me. And what a beautiful lesson to carry over into every area of my life, particularly my love life. The weeks when I lost my grandmother and John but found my new home had increased my faith so much as I watched God carry me through the valleys and make a way for me on the mountain. It was truly time for a new chapter. A much-needed new chapter. In the past, I had always run from change, but now I was learning to embrace it with arms wide-open, because I now trusted that my every step was being ordered by God.

Before too long, my last day in apartment 33 arrived. Shannon came over to help me pack and also to help me say goodbye. Not just to the apartment and to The Boy Upstairs but to the person I'd been there. Because true friends sit with you on boxes in your packed-up apartment and eat pizza from paper plates and let you ramble on about all your many memories from the past two years within those four walls that after tomorrow will no longer be home. (Sometimes letting go is just a little easier when you have someone holding your hand.)

But to open your hands and your heart and your life to the new, you must first release and pay a proper goodbye to the old.

My time in apartment 33 had been bittersweet. Leaving it felt much like living in it did: Uncertain. A little scary. Exciting. I was nostalgic. Relieved. Happy. Sad.

I tend to be a bit of a wanderer when it comes to my home base. I usually never stay in an apartment for more than a year. I get bored and uninspired by my surroundings and need to move on. But this place...

This place had been my home for the past two years. Longer than anywhere I'd stayed in quite some time. And I was a vastly different woman going than I was coming.

My family experienced the greatest tragedy we'd ever faced while I lived at that apartment. I had to sit my nieces down on the couch and explain that their daddy had been in an accident and we weren't sure when he was coming home.

I released my third book at that apartment. One entire wall there was once filled with a giant dream board, with my readers' biggest goals and hopes and plans posted on it.

I left my publisher and ventured into the unknown at that apartment. I was still figuring out exactly where my career path and my writing was going...one step, one day at a time. Nothing was yet clear. But then again: When nothing is certain, anything is possible, right?

I battled the biggest fight of my life with anxiety and depression at that apartment. And I won.

I started dating again for the first time in more than two years at that apartment. Opened up my heart again. Took chances on love again. Lost a few times...but I wouldn't be where and who I was if I hadn't lowered the walls and let people in again. I might be more broken because of it, but I liked to think my scattered pieces were more brave and beautiful than any sturdy wall could ever be.

I lost my precious grandmother while I lived at that apartment. I whispered a last, most beloved prayer of mine in her ear to take straight to Jesus...not knowing it would be the last words I would ever speak to her on this earth.

I made friends while I lived at apartment 33 that I knew would be with me for life. I lost friends there that

I thought would be with me for life. I cried, I fought, I clawed and scratched and struggled just to hold on... then I cried and fought and clawed and scratched and struggled to let go. I shed parts of me there... some parts I missed and some I hoped to never see again. I BECAME there. I LIVED there.

For a long time, I wasn't living; I was hiding out. Protecting myself. Guarding my heart from pain and cracks and loss. Not realizing that pain and cracks and loss are all a part of being ALIVE. Of being brave. Of being wholehearted. Of being on the front lines rather than sitting back in a protective bubble, watching the world pass you by. I never want to live a sheltered, safe existence again. Every moment of the crazy, tragic, sometimes almost magic story that had played out within those four walls over the past two years had taught me that.

Apartment 33 had made me... a little more ME.

But now it was time to go.

You Are Enough

For a really long time... almost a year... I didn't even like going home. I associated my apartment with the string of disappointments and heartbreaks that had happened in my life. I didn't date for years, and then all within a matter of a year, two different guys drifted in and out of my life and my home and left scars on my heart. Because of memories associated with those relationships combined with the struggles I went through, I got to the point where I avoided home at all costs. I stayed on the go nonstop for almost a year...like a whirlwind, never pausing long enough to reflect or relax or restore my weary soul...because if I stopped even for a moment, the sadness and the hurt from the memories in that apartment caught up to me. I wore myself out with constant activity and forward motion. Much like a hamster in a wheel, I was constantly moving but going nowhere.

When I moved into my new home, that all changed. My new home was, well...HOME. It was like a tranquil oasis of calm and peace and comfort. It was warm and cozy and so very restorative to my soul. I never fully grasped the importance of loving your surroundings until I experienced it myself, and now I see how important it is to live somewhere that brings you joy. This place brings me joy. I never want to leave home now, and I can't even express how wonderful that feels after feeling so disconnected from my surroundings. It's a beautiful thing to feel like everything in your life is just as it should be, even your living environment. It is so perfectly enough. I think maybe I had to reach the place where I realized that I was enough before I could find the place that felt like enough to contain the new version of me. It brought me incredible peace to have my outside finally match my insides.

Peace is a beautiful thing. Pursue it at all costs. Keep nothing around you, object or relationship, that robs you of your peace and contentment. And don't be afraid to leave the place where you've found yourself if it doesn't feel like home, if it doesn't feel like enough for the you that you are becoming. A few months ago, I would have been desperately seeking any reason to escape my apartment, the ghosts that haunted me there, and the empty feeling of never quite measuring up to what those ghosts wanted. But tonight I sit on my couch listening to crickets chirp outside my window with nothing but peace in my heart. It took me a very long time to get here, but every step was worth the destination.

Because I can finally say...

It. Is. Well.

chapter 18

CHURCH CHASERS

I opened the Bible app on my phone to look up a verse one day not too long after my move and noticed that the last time I was active on the app had been thirty-eight weeks earlier. So, of course, then I had to look and see what was happening in my life thirty-eight weeks prior. When I did, I was taken back to what felt like an entire lifetime ago. I remembered exactly where I was and what I was doing. What I was on the cusp of. The people I was about to meet. The things, both good and bad, I was about to experience. Isn't it funny how the very things that take you away from God are the very same things that push you back to Him once they're gone?

I had opened my Bible app that day more than six

months earlier just like every other morning. But I'd had no idea that I wouldn't open it again for thirty-eight weeks. The Mandy who closed the app thirty-eight weeks earlier was not the same Mandy who reopened it. Was I grateful for that? I think so. I don't know that I'd change anything, because if I did...if I did even one tiny thing differently...I might not have gotten lost in the direction that I had. And then I might not have gotten found in the way that I had. And funnily enough, out there in the wilderness, I stumbled across some truly beautiful things and people.

The last verse I had highlighted thirty-eight weeks prior was 1 Corinthians 13:12: "We don't yet see things clearly. We're squinting in a fog, peering through a mist. But it won't be long before the weather clears and the sun shines bright! We'll see it all then, see it all as clearly as God sees us, knowing him directly just as he knows us!" (MSG) I loved that this was the last Scripture I had highlighted, because I had spent the greater part of the past thirty-eight weeks squinting into the fog and peering through the mist. But now it was finally starting to feel like the weather was clearing and the sun was shining again. And thirty-eight-weeks-later me was grateful to be coming out of the storms, but equally grateful for the strength and clarity the storms brought me.

I had reached a place of peace with almost every area of my life. I had come through intensive therapy that brought me a sense of wholeness and belonging that I had never had before. I had made some of the best friends of my life. I had closed the door on John, once and for all. And I had moved away from The Boy Upstairs and the shadows of the past and into a home that I absolutely loved. My life felt like it was finally ENOUGH. Almost.

Spiritually, I was still somewhat adrift. I was praying and trying to seek God and strengthen my relationship with Him again, but I still wasn't sure if I was ready to return to church. So much about the current church culture turned me off. I hadn't felt or seen Jesus in any church I had been to in a very long time. And I was still not completely recovered from a painful experience I'd had at the church I attended in my early twenties. I served and served and served the church because that was what was expected of me. And in the process, I lost sight of what it meant to simply serve God. Eventually, it started to feel like nothing I did was good enough for the church leaders, and in turn, nothing was enough for God. Once again, my feelings of inadequacy and never feeling like I was ENOUGH reared their ugly heads.

It occurred to me that perhaps it was time for a change. I had spent the majority of my time as a Christian in contemporary charismatic churches. Maybe I just needed to experience something different for a while. Maybe I needed to become a church chaser!

I enlisted my friend Jen in this adventure, and we decided to visit a different church every week, all denominations and traditions and sizes, until we each found our place. I was excited to see the different facets of Jesus that

I might discover within the different places. I wasn't the same person I was the last time I attended church regularly, so why should my experience stay the same? It was time for new wineskins and new encounters. Who knew what I might discover about Him, and about myself, in this quest? I'd had enough of the same old "sing a few songs, raise your hands, laugh at the jokes of the pastor (who's probably wearing skinny jeans), stop by the coffee bar on your way out, and call it a day" experiences. I wanted something deeper. Something more real and raw and authentic. Something I wasn't sure existed, but I was willing and ready to test the waters and see what was out there.

The first church Jen and I visited was Episcopalian. I had never been to an Episcopalian church, so it was an entirely new experience for me. It was very formal, but I found moments of great beauty and comfort in the rituals. Kneeling to pray, the sign of the cross, the confessing of sins, the recitations; I got teary eyed during one of the readings that talked about Jesus and His sacrifice on the cross, because we're not often enough reminded of that in the current culture of feel-good self-help messaging that comes from our more contemporary pulpits. I decided that the Episcopalian church wasn't my place but that it was really nice and eye-opening to see people experience Jesus in such a different way from what I was accustomed to. It was nice to be reminded that He's still there in the hymnals; He's still there in that "old-time religion"; He's still there in the traditions. He's always there. (He's even there in the skinny-jeans culture as well.)

The next place we visited was a tiny country church out by the ranch where I used to live. I would pass by the church every single day and always enjoyed the powerful messages on its little sign. Something about the church always called to me, but I never made it a point to visit until then. Quite by coincidence (or not, because nothing really is a coincidence) a couple of weeks prior, my dad had mentioned that he knew the pastor there and had been wanting to visit. So I took that as a sign, and finally entered the doors of the church I had driven past so many times before.

I entered with my spiritually wounded heart and more than a few preconceived notions. Tiny country churches don't tend to be the most open-minded, and I wasn't in the headspace to hear rantings about hellfire and brimstone. I was still too raw and vulnerable in that regard when it came to my faith. I didn't want to hear about the wrath of God—I needed to hear about His grace. I needed to know that He still loved me even though I had strayed from Him for a season. I needed to hear that I was enough for Him, absentee churchgoer for two years and all.

I underestimated that little house of worship. Vastly.

First of all, I should say we were two of only about twenty-five people in the entire church. Translation: We stood out. So much so that after the first couple of worship songs, the pastor asked us to stand up in front of the congregation and introduce ourselves. In more than thirty years of churching, I've never had to do that. It felt a little awkward, but we rolled with it. The comforting old hymns we sang took me back to my childhood, and when the few children in attendance stood to sing "This Little Light of Mine," it brought tears to my eyes. There was something very grounding and centering about experiencing the traditions of my Baptist youth, which surprised me. I had attended contemporary churches for so long I had forgotten how beautiful it can be to go back to basics.

But the biggest surprise came for me in the pastor's message. He was a good old Southern boy, as country as corn bread. And yet, spoken and sometimes shouted in his rich Southern twang from that little pulpit was a message of inclusiveness and openness and love. The essence of the message was this: Anyone is welcome into the kingdom of heaven. Anyone. Jesus didn't come for the saint; He came for the sinner. And the biggest sinners of all are the ones who think they have a bigger claim on God because they are "better" or less sinful than anyone else. The message was like Chicken Soup for the Soul of the broken and imperfect. It was exactly what my heart needed in that moment. And it was good.

That little country church, quite off the beaten path along a Tennessee back road, might not have ultimately been my church home, but it reminded me to not judge a book by its cover. To remain open to what God wants to do, even if it comes wrapped in a package you weren't expecting and didn't even order. And that sometimes coming home to God means coming home to your roots, if only for an hour or two.

From there, we visited a Lutheran church. A Methodist church. A Unity church (which I loved)! We churched our way across Middle Tennessee, and one afternoon we even stopped by a Buddhist temple. Now don't start clutching your pearls or anything. We hadn't decided to become Buddhists. We just wanted to see FAITH through the eyes of a completely different culture. And I have to say, though I didn't feel any spiritual presence there, I was quite moved by some of the offerings people had left at the statue of Buddha. It takes audacity to believe in a higher power, even if it's not the one I happen to believe in.

Our church chasing culminated in a trip to a Catholic monastery in Cullman, Alabama. It was a place I had heard about years ago from my former editor and had been longing to visit ever since. The monks there welcome visitors to come stay with them, literally inside the monastery. You can attend prayer and Mass and meals with the monks, though most everything is done in silence. I had never been to a Catholic Mass, but I had always been somewhat fascinated by the Catholic faith, with its confessionals and rosaries and reverence. There is something very beautiful to me about the rich tradition of it all.

And there was something very beautiful about the monastery where we would be spending the weekend.

Rolling hills, historic structures and statues, gorgeous walking trails, and all of it blanketed in the most peaceful, holy silence I have ever heard in my life. Yes, it was the kind of silence you could hear and feel, right down to your very soul.

Over the past few months, I had spent so much time talking...over the past few years, really...talking in group therapy and talking in individual therapy and talking to friends and talking about my problems and talking about every detail of my life on my blog and in my books. Talking and talking and talking until I was completely and totally talked out. It was time to get really, really silent. It was time to let God fill up the space created by that silence.

And He did.

I don't really know how to explain what happened at that monastery on that hot August weekend in 2017, but I can say that I felt, little by little, pieces of my spirit that had been lost for some time start to fall back into place. Over those two days among the silence and the beauty of that holy ground, I felt something click. Something big. Something inherently ME. The old Mandy. The Mandy that had great faith and trust in God and His plan for her life. She had been reawakened. Resurrected. Restored. Reinvigorated. All those *Where is God in all this?* moments over the past two years suddenly came into focus. He had been right there all along. He just needed me to come to the end of myself to see it.

My weekend spent among the monks, who became

my silent teachers and friends, taught me that life doesn't have to be so complicated and dramatic and hard. It can be simple and pure and minimalist and still be wonderfully, perfectly ENOUGH. The monks lead simple, structured lives. Their number one priority in everything they do is God. My number one priority for so long had been myself, and figuring out and sorting through my overly complicated life. Sometimes merely surviving the day had taken every last ounce of my energy.

It was time to take a deep breath and let all of that go. It was time to get back to the basics. Of me, and of life. It was time to surrender. It was time to accept, once and for all, that God was enough. That my life was enough. That I was enough.

I'm still searching for my church home. I know I'll find it. Until then, I'm content with finding new facets of God in new places. That's what letting go does, what surrendering allows you to do: release the old to make room for the new.

You Are Enough

It's a spiritual practice, the letting go. I realized that the past two years had been about me clinging to my will and my plans and my people with clenched fists. Keeping myself so busy with activities and plans that

I'd had no time to even sit and ponder what God's plan for my life might be. I'd been completely bypassing His will for my own. Busyness had become my idol. The merry-go-round of avoidance had allowed me to crowd out sadness and aloneness and time to think. But it had also crowded out God. It had crowded out creativity. It had crowded out growth and change and forward movement. It had kept me stuck. And I didn't want to be stuck. In order to move forward, we have to give God room to move in our lives. What does that look like? It looks a lot like letting go. Like surrendering. Like slowing down. There comes a point when it's time to stop frantically pursuing our own will and our own plans and simply get out of the way and let Him move.

So I say, let it all go. Trust that whatever and whoever are meant for us will stick. And whatever is not will go. And in that space...that beautiful, scary, empty space...new life and new plans and new beginnings and new people will emerge.

And it will be enough.

chapter 19

NO ONE ELSE CAN LEAVE

My life, which had fallen apart completely, was finally coming back together. This new Mandy—the way the pieces were being put back together—felt good. It felt right. It felt...complete. I wasn't perfect, and I would never be. The perfect friend, the perfect daughter, the perfect sister, the perfect writer, the perfect Christian: That wasn't me, and I was at peace with that. Perhaps for the first time ever in my life. The burden I had been carrying around for years, that I wasn't enough, had finally lifted. I may not be EVERYTHING...but I was enough. (And I had the tattoo on my wrist to prove it.)

I had decided to take the summer off from dating or trying to make any kind of romantic connection, and to allow myself to heal from the wounds left by John and The Boy Upstairs. And, of course, the wounds left by me. I was often the biggest damager of my soul, with my constant negative self-talk and my penchant for carrying the failure of every relationship I had ever had on my shoulders. I needed a break from my search for love. I wanted to get back to the basics of life and focus on my friendships and my faith and my future as a writer. I was in talks with a new publisher (about this book!), and things seemed to be coming together on the career front. I was in a great place with God. And I was having arguably the best summer of my life with my girlfriends.

There was this one really beautiful night that stands out to me now, when Shannon and Grace and our friend Michelle and I decided to go out dancing. It was during the CMA Music Festival, so downtown Nashville was complete chaos. But we danced it out anyway, and ate pizza, people-watched, and listened to live music while sitting in the middle of Lower Broadway—literally in the middle of the street. Then we stumbled upon the most hilarious Uber driver ever, who danced it out with us when he dropped us back off at our cars in an empty parking lot. Nobody was quite ready to go home yet, so we all sat there in a circle on the warm pavement, talking about life in the shadow of the Nashville skyline. And I didn't wind up crawling into bed until three in the morning (which is far more painful in your thirties than it is in your twenties), but it didn't matter, because this was my life and I had come to see how it was magical and wondrous and, yes, sometimes painful but oh so very ENOUGH. And although I might still be a little broken, when you find those people whose broken pieces fit yours, it is a beautiful thing.

That night stands out to me now because it was the last time I ever saw Grace.

My precious friend Gracie. The girl whose smile lit up every room and whose laugh made the whole world just seem like a brighter place. The girl who loved unicorns and loved to dance and who brought me a teddy bear on Valentine's Day because she knew I was sad about being single for yet another V-Day. The girl who completed my circle. The girl who felt like part of my family. My sister.

I got the call at four o'clock on a Saturday morning. It was Grace's boyfriend, James. "Grace is gone," he said.

I sat up in bed, confused. "What do you mean, gone? Is she missing?"

"No. She's gone. She took her life tonight."

My heart started pounding out of my chest. I tried frantically to make sense of what he was saying. I had just texted her a few days ago. She was supposed to go on a kayaking trip with us in a couple of weeks. How could she be gone?

I asked James for all the details. I needed him to explain what had happened, so that I could understand. I needed him to make me understand. Not that anything he could have said would help me grasp the immense loss of a beautiful, intelligent, hilarious, bighearted twenty-three-year-old who had barely even begun her life. And now it was over.

James said Grace had been really struggling lately. I don't think any of us fully grasped the depth of how badly she was struggling. She had been back in the hospital for a few days, and when she got out, the first chance she got she slipped away from her family, who was keeping watch over her, and she ended it. Just like that. In the blink of an eye. Our beautiful friend was gone.

It took me back to my darkest moments a few months earlier. Reminded me of just how close I had been to the edge myself. Though I had never made or attempted to execute a plan to end my life, there were definitely days when I didn't want to go on. Wasn't sure I could go on. By the grace of God, I had made it through. I was on the other side. But Gracie hadn't, and wasn't, and now . . . would never be.

She was gone.

I had to be the one to break the news to Shannon and Michelle and some of our other group family. We all spent most of that day on the phone together, crying and mourning and remembering our dear friend. Struggling to understand. Trying not to blame ourselves for not being able to save her. We couldn't have. No one could have. Gracie didn't take her life—depression did. The same as if she had passed away from cancer or a heart attack or some other fatal disease. Depression is the cruelest of silent killers.

Several months before, a group of us had gone with

Grace as she got the word "warrior" tattooed on her side. Make no mistake about it: Grace WAS a warrior, right up until the moment she died. Anyone who fights and claws and struggles to battle their way back from depression and suicidal thoughts time and time and time again IS a warrior. She was just so tired she couldn't fight anymore. I guess even warriors have their limits.

We all gathered for a somber dinner that night, at our version of Cheers, a place called Pancho's, right down the road from Whispering Pines. It was the same place we always went to celebrate someone's graduation from group therapy. Now we were there to remember our fallen comrade. To hug each other. To grieve. And to remind one another that NO ONE ELSE CAN LEAVE.

This would become our refrain from that day forward, both when we saw one another and in text-message conversations. NO ONE ELSE CAN LEAVE. No matter what happens, that was our pact. We were in this life thing together. No matter how hard it might get. No one else can leave.

And now I say that to you, too. My precious friend wanted to go. She saw no other way out. And although there is nothing I can do now to save her...I can still perhaps make an impact on someone else who is reading this and questioning whether or not they want to stay. NO ONE ELSE CAN LEAVE. You must fight to stay. Fight with everything you have in you, and realize that depression is screwing with your brain and wants to kill you, BUT YOU MUST NOT LET IT. Reach out. Ask for help. Talk to someone, anyone. A friend. A family member. A pastor. You are not alone, even though your disease wants to convince you that you are. It does and WILL get better. I am living proof of that. I haven't always been a poster child for mental wellness, by any means, but I have now battled my way back from severe, crippling depression multiple times in my life. And you can, too.

A week or so later, we all gathered together once again to say our final goodbyes to Grace. There were a lot of tears…but also a lot of smiles…remembering our girl with some of her favorite things: unicorns and cupcakes (Shannon even came decked out in a unicorn onesie). I bet Grace really loved it. And as we released our balloons and watched them float up to heaven, I felt certain they were floating right from our hands to hers.

Grace's parents and brother showed up for our memorial and, through their own tears and grief, somehow found a way to comfort us. They listened to our stories and memories of Grace and shared their own. And before he left that day, her dad said something to us that I will never forget: "You all have found something very special here. Hold on to it. Take care of each other."

This little motley crew, this little family we built for ourselves, would never be quite complete again without Grace. There would always be something missing. But we will carry her with us forever. Her smile. Her way of looking within you and calling out the good when you saw nothing but the bad. Her silliness. Her heart. Her laughter. It's all still here with us—maybe not as close as we'd like it to be, but imprinted on all of our hearts forevermore.

I love you, little unicorn. Fly high until we meet again someday.

You Are Enough

I know now that from this day forward it will be my mission in life to speak out against this cruel disease known as depression and this heartbreaking epidemic called suicide.

If you are suffering from suicidal thoughts, please ask for help. There are so many resources out there. You can find a complete list of some of my favorites at the back of this book.

Please hear me, dear one: NO ONE ELSE CAN LEAVE. You mustn't throw in the towel. There is great meaning to your life and a completely unique assignment for you to fulfill. Without you, something truly precious and needed would be missing from the world. So keep going, you perfectly imperfect, inevitably flawed, gloriously beautiful, breathtaking mess of a human, you. You are loved. You are enough. You have inherent value. And you are infinitely more important than you may ever know.

As I said in the very front of this book:

Keep going.

Keep going.

Keep going.

You are a semicolon; you are not a period.

chapter 20

LET IT BE

*G*race was gone. The summer was almost gone.

I had lost many things over the past year—love and friendship, Nanny and Grace, John and The Boy Upstairs. Some to death, some to circumstance.

I had also lost some things that I wasn't sad to see go—like the nagging sense of self-doubt that seemed to follow me wherever I went. My feelings of unworthiness. My broken heart. Loneliness. The voice in my head that told me for so long that I simply wasn't enough.

It was time to celebrate what remained.

Shannon, Michelle, Alex, and I had planned a kayaking trip to West Tennessee a few weeks earlier. Grace was originally supposed to come with us. Now it would just be the four of us staying at the cozy little cabin on the beautiful little creek in the middle of nowhere.

I think we were all excited to get away and have a couple of days of carefree abandon. We had been in mourning for weeks, and we all desperately needed to just be together and laugh and to celebrate our friendship and life and how far we had all come since we had met eight months earlier. Plus I had never been kayaking before, and though I was a little anxious to be out of my comfort zone, I was also excited for a new adventure.

The first night was blissfully relaxed and the perfect way to ease into our weekend. We lounged around the cabin, grilled out, watched a chick flick, and staged a dance party on our giant deck, which overlooked the creek. We shared funny stories and favorite memories about Grace. We acted goofy and ate copious amounts of junk food and giggled until our faces hurt.

Day two at the creek dawned bright and early. It was kayaking time! The float down the creek would take us about six hours. We showed up armed with coolers of drinks and snacks (and being the ever-prepared worrier of the group, I made sure we had plenty of water and sunblock, too). We were ready to go!

I don't know if you've ever been kayaking before, but it was the most fun I've ever had in my life. The creek was fairly shallow and calm, so we didn't run into any rough waters. And I'm proud to say I managed to stay in my kayak with no tip-overs the entire day! (The same can't be said for poor Alex, who somehow managed to lose both her kayak and one of her paddles at one point.)

Sometimes we would float alongside one another, and other times we would be separated for a bit and I would be left to breathe in the serenity of the creek, the glorious nature, the sun, the panoramic views, and the peaceful silence. I had moments of sheer bliss that day. I was surrounded by my best friends, I felt God's presence around every corner, and I had made it through the most heartbreaking, challenging, bittersweet, strangely beautiful year of my life.

At some point during that second day, one of the four of us suggested that we should get matching tattoos to commemorate not just our weekend, but our friendships. A quick sidebar about tattoos. I know some people don't like or agree with them. Some people even believe tattooing your body is an affront to God. My parents hate my tattoos. I get it. Tattoos aren't for everyone. But I personally find most tattoos to be beautiful and artistic and a unique way of forever immortalizing a significant season or moment or event or person in your life.

To my group therapy family, tattoos were hugely meaningful. Most of us had at least a few. I think when you go through hard things in life like we had all been through—losing people, losing faith, losing yourself—you want to find a way to celebrate when you make it out on the other side. Because some of us hadn't made it out on the other side. Tattoos seemed to be our way of celebrating. It's audacious, really, to mark yourself with something that you know will be with you forever. It makes you feel like even though life isn't infinite, perhaps you can be. Perhaps friendship can be.

So that day when someone suggested we get matching tattoos, the rest of us quickly agreed. Our tattoos would link us forever. Our bond would be cemented. Regardless of where our lives would take us, we could always look down at those tattoos and remember this weekend, these moments, these people. The ones who stood by us when it felt like the rest of the world had left. The keepers of our darkest days. The witnesses to both our descent and our rising. It was perfect.

We batted around various ideas of what we should get. Everyone tossed out suggestions. Nothing felt quite right.

Then suddenly, as I was sitting there in the middle of the creek in my kayak, gazing out at the expanse of water before me, it came to me. I can remember the exact moment that it hit me almost from nowhere. Divine inspiration at its finest.

"I know," I exclaimed. "We should get the words 'let it be' tattooed on our foot!"

I loved this phrase, this song, this message. I always had. But I'd never shared that with any of my girlfriends before.

As soon as the words left my mouth, Shannon started crying. I heard the sobs, so I quickly turned my kayak around to see what was wrong.

"Shannon? What is it?" I asked, worried.

For a moment she couldn't speak.

Then, through her tears, she said: "That's the exact tattoo that Lucy wanted. In the exact spot."

Lucy. Shannon's precious daughter. Her beautiful, talented, spunky seventeen-year-old daughter, who had taken her own life a year and a half earlier because she was being bullied at school and couldn't take it anymore. Shannon never knew about the bullying until it was too late. Lucy was gone and now all Shannon and her husband could do was to try desperately to pick up the pieces of their lives and try to build something meaningful for their two little boys. Something that would never quite feel whole, or the same, or even good. But something real. Something that might not be everything, but it would be enough. Because it had to be.

Except Lucy wasn't really gone, because at that moment in the middle of the creek, the four of us knew that she was there with us. We felt her spirit there, dancing among the trees and the dragonflies and the sunshine. She was with us.

Just like Nanny. Just like Grace.

I paddled my way over to Shannon, and we sat for a long moment, awkwardly hugging as best we could from one kayak to the other, both of us with tears streaming down our faces.

We both knew...the four of us knew...that it was right. It was time to let it be. To let it all be. Not to let it all go, necessarily, but to let it be. Peace, be still. To stop striving and simply KNOW. Know that He is God, know that we are enough, know that our lives might never be the same as they once were, with all the missing pieces of us gone, but that they could still be something meaningful. They could still be ENOUGH.

After we got back from our float, we managed to find a little tattoo parlor nearby—yes, in the middle of nowhere—that could fit us all in. (It's a wonder our feet didn't fall off, but thankfully, I can report, more than a year later, all eight feet are present and accounted for.) And the really crazy twist to the story? When we got there, we were telling the tattoo artist what we wanted when he broke out into laughter. We all looked at each other quizzically. He said, "Follow me. You have to see this."

There, on his computer screen, in his office, was a picture of a tattoo that read "let it be." It had been his first tattoo of the day, and he thought it was so pretty he saved it as his screen saver. Now it would be his last tattoo of the day, too. A magical bookend to close a magical weekend.

Just like this book starts and ends with a tattoo.

When I was going through my social media archives the other night to refresh my memories about our kayaking weekend so I could write this chapter, I was struck by the smile on my face in the pictures and videos. That smile wasn't there for the longest time. For a little while, I thought it might never be there again. I thought about how I wish I could turn back the clock a few months and go tell that Mandy that her smile isn't going to be missing forever. I wish I could tell her to hang in there . . . because happy, silly, carefree moments are going to come again.

I wish I could tell her to keep pushing and fighting and showing up to her life and doing the hard work every day, because eventually everything that's shifting on the inside will show up on the outside. Eventually, the darkness will give way to light. I wish I could tell her that there will be moments ahead that take her breath away, from the sheer beauty instead of the sheer pain.

I wish I could tell her that losing herself was just another step to finding herself. I wish I could tell her that she was ENOUGH, just as she was then, and she would continue to be enough, even if she never changed a thing.

But I can't. I can't go back in time. What I *can* do is choose to smile and dance on and look back at all versions of me with fondness and gratitude that I am ever shifting, ever changing, ever evolving—and recognize how glorious the ebb and flow of life is, indeed.

At the beginning of this journey, I declared my "enoughness" with a tattoo on my wrist. And now it was time to accept that enoughness and let it be. Let where I had been be. Let who and what I had lost be. Let my former life be. My new life may not be perfect—I may not be perfect—but it was enough. I was enough.

I was completely, totally, at peace with my humanness.

Lord knows I struggle and flounder and wander aimlessly at times. I fight to become the woman I'm meant to be, and I fight against letting go of the woman I used to be all at the same time. I make mistakes and question everything and walk in anxiety far more often than I walk in faith...

But I love big and I love hard and I am fiercely loyal and crazy passionate, and if I'm riding with you, you've got a ride-or-die friend for life.

I bring the broken and sweaty and messy and imperfect, because that's exactly what this life is: broken and sweaty and messy and imperfect.

I'm gorgeously human.

Flawed and fabulous.

And I am ENOUGH.

You are enough.

It's time for us to accept that.

And then ...

Let it be.

You Are Enough

Maybe the happy ending is moving on instead of holding on. Maybe the happy ending is losing yourself in order to find yourself. Maybe the happy ending is just letting it be. Maybe the happy ending is realizing that your life might be writing a story completely different from the one you had planned. Maybe the happy ending is deciding to enjoy the breathtaking beauty of the sunset, whether you're riding off into it alone or with someone by your side. Maybe the happy ending is simply being happy no matter who or what comes—or doesn't come—your way. Maybe the happy ending is seeing that you were strong enough to handle whatever life threw your way. Maybe the happy ending is simply that you're still standing at the end of the day. Maybe the happy ending is choosing YOUR-SELF at the end of the movie. Maybe the happy ending is accepting yourself for exactly who you are in all your forms: The Heartbroken One. The Healing One. The Whole One.

Or maybe the happy ending is realizing that no matter which one of those versions of yourself you happen to be at any given moment...you are enough. You always were.

You always will be.

epilogue

THE JOURNEY TO "ENOUGH"
IS NEVER OVER

*M*y publisher asked me a few weeks after the manuscript for this book was complete if I felt like I had one more chapter in me, just to make the book you're currently holding in your hands a bit lengthier. I said, "No, I sure don't. I feel like it's perfect as is. It's tied up nicely, with a neat little bow, and good to go. I can't possibly add another word!"

But then I gave it a few days of reflection and I realized I did have something more to say.

The journey to feeling like "enough" is never over. I don't want anyone to read this book and see a nice story and a perfect little arc and feel like just because my story ended on a positive note that I've somehow achieved a level of self-awareness and completeness that you yourself can never attain. Believe me, I know how elusive "enough" can feel. Even after I stopped typing this story and closed my computer screen, I still have days when I don't feel like I'm enough. That's why I tattooed the word "enough" on my wrist, because I know better than anyone how you can feel like enough today and feel like nothing tomorrow. And that's also why I wrote this book, so that on those days when I'm feeling like nothing and you're feeling like nothing, we can come back to these pages and remind ourselves that we aren't nothing. We aren't even just something. We are EVERYTHING.

You can't tie up a book about enoughness with a neat little bow. You just can't. It's not a goal to be checked off a bucket list. It's not a state that you achieve and then never question your self-worth again. Because here's the thing: You can be grounded in who you are and be confident in who God created you to be and still be sent reeling by a hurt, a heartbreak, a rejection. Guys are still going to break our hearts. People we love are still going to die. Disappointment is going to come. Loss is inevitable. Pain is inevitable. If I learned anything over the course of the two years documented in this book, it's that life has a beautiful, terrible give-and-take. Today's joy can be tomorrow's sorrow. Today's scar can be tomorrow's wound. And today's full can be tomorrow's empty.

But by that same logic, today's tears can be tomorrow's laughter. Today's goodbye can be tomorrow's hello.

epilogue

And today's glass half empty can be tomorrow's cup runneth over. You've just gotta stay the course, and TRUST. Keep fighting. KEEP FIGHTING. Keep fighting for your healing. Keep fighting for your wholeness. Keep fighting for your enoughness. And realize that the fighter inside of you who has refused to throw in the towel against all odds—anxiety, depression, loss, heartbreak, pain, disappointment, your past, etc.—man, is that person ever worth loving.

I used to think that in order to be enough, I had to be perfect. Hair in place, details in place, LIFE in place. Now I know that being enough means simply accepting myself, in this moment, just as I am, work in progress and all. If we wait until everything is perfect to love ourselves, we won't ever love ourselves, because life isn't meant to be perfect. It's messy, and it's complicated, and it's sometimes very hard. And that's okay. It is still enough. WE are still enough. So wherever you're at in your journey... I hope you embrace it with both arms wide-open. You will always be unfinished, and you know what? That's okay. That's called *growing*. Evolving. Becoming. That's called being brave enough to surrender the perfect finished portrait for the messy, constantly changing finger-painted one. Being brave enough to risk the heartbreaks of life in order to realize the healing and wholeness on the other side.

Keep clinging to the knowledge that YOU ARE ENOUGH. Even on those days when you feel like you're not—your enoughness doesn't go away just because you can't see it or feel it right at this moment. It's there. It's always been there. It just might take you, you beautifully broken, sensitive soul, a little longer to see in yourself what everyone else already knows: that you are growing, and learning, and changing, and trying, and seeking, and healing, and striving, and thriving...and you are simply, perfectly, wonderfully, beautifully ENOUGH.

with gratitude

I would like to thank the wonderful team at FaithWords / Hachette Book Group, especially Keren Baltzer, for helping me bring this book to life. This is, I feel, the most important book I've ever written, and it wouldn't have been possible without the team's belief in me and my message.

I'd like to thank my family for always being there for me through the good times and bad. For never giving up on me. And for reminding me that I'm enough during those times when I've forgotten.

And finally—I'd like to thank my readers. You've stood by me for almost a decade now, through all the many twists and turns of my journey. Being a small part of your lives has been one of the most rewarding experiences of mine. Thank you for growing with me, for always cheering me on, and for sharing your hearts and stories with me over the years. You are my sisters, my friends, my inspiration, and I love you all.

This book is in memory of my precious grandmother, Emily Jean Reed Frost, a.k.a. Nanny.

appendix

Resources for Suicide Prevention

This is by no means an exhaustive list; however, these are some of the resources that have helped me and people close to me:

National Suicide Prevention Lifeline:
1-800-273-8255 / SuicidePreventionLifeline.org
American Foundation for Suicide Prevention: AFSP.org
Crisis Text Line: 741741 (Text) / CrisisTextLine.org
To Write Love on Her Arms: TWLOHA.com
The Trevor Project: 1-866-488-7386 / TheTrevorProject.org
Hope For The Day: HFTD.org
Buddy Project: Buddy-Project.org

Please tell someone that you're suffering. There IS help for you. There IS hope for you. It does get better. No one else can leave.

about the author

Blogger turned *New York Times* bestselling author and speaker **Mandy Hale** is the creator of The Single Woman brand, books, blog, and social media platforms. Mandy has spent almost a decade inspiring millions of single women across the world to live their best, most empowered lives. Mandy is a believer, a dreamer, a nature lover, a self-professed book/TV/movie nerd, and a mental health advocate. You can connect with her online at MandyHale.com.